and Church Wilne

by Richard Guise

NEDDYTOWN
Copyright © Richard Guise, 2001
Second edition (for print by www.lulu.com) © Richard Guise, 2014
All rights reserved
Cover design: Richard Guise
Cover photographs: Long Eaton Library
Published by Richard Guise
Printed by www.lulu.com
ISBN: 978-1-291-73652-6

The maps included in this book are merely for illustration of points made in the text and hence their accuracy cannot be guaranteed. They should therefore not be used for any other purpose.

ACKNOWLEDGEMENTS

Many local people have contributed their time, advice, knowledge and memories to this book and I hope I haven't forgotten any in the following list.

Thanks to Joyce Barton, David Brown (of Erewash Borough Council's Technical Services Department), Mary Burrows, Florence Clay, George Clay, Raymond Coulson, Andrew Disney (of the Environment Agency), Barry Fletcher, Grace Gaskin, John Higton, Mike Joblin (of Long Eaton Library), Val Lewis (Draycott Parish Clerk), Alysn Midgelow-Marsden, Lou Haywood, Margaret Orchard, Terry Springthorpe, Tony Wall, Lillian Wheeldon, Paul White and Colette White.

Finally, I owe special thanks to Janet Shaw for reviewing the entire text (though any remaining errors are naturally my responsibility!); to Max and Julie Alexander for opening so many local doors, as it were; and to Derek Orchard and Ron Mason, who have both been outstanding sources of information, enthusiasm and encouragement.

RGG
June 2001

Contents

1. Crawling Through Neddytown...5
2. Crossing Points (Before 1100)..10
3. Country Villages (1100 – 1800)..22
4. Industrial Outposts (1800 – 1907)...34
5. All Hands to the Pump (1908 – 1953)...52
6. Commuter Territory (1954 – 2000)...67
7. Answers to the 'History Mysteries'...84
8. Bibliography...86

1. Crawling Through Neddytown

Draycott? A history??! Driving through this elongated South Derbyshire village on a wet Wednesday afternoon, you might be forgiven for thinking that it probably just emerged spontaneously from a grey suburban swamp and can't really have had a history at all. Well, I hope this book shows that there's more to Draycott – and *a lot* more to Church Wilne – than now meets the 21st-century eye.

Your first question may be: why 'Neddytown'? Well, along with some other intriguing local mysteries, this introduction will pose the question and then let you discover the answer as you read. (If you want to cheat, all the answers are towards the end of the book.) To the inhabitants of the surrounding towns and villages, Draycott has indeed been known for some time as Neddytown – and its inhabitants as Neddies, a nickname that usually carries – how shall we put it? – somewhat less than complimentary overtones. But where did the name come from? (History Mystery 1)

Before we start the tale, let's attempt an image makeover for the sake of the outsider whose impression of Draycott may not be too positive. Certainly, with December's lumbering skies pressed close to the drabber corners of the village, and the bare trees of winter ruthlessly exposing all grim, grey shades to a critical gaze, this is no Côte d'Azur. However, apart from those settlements blessed with a castle, a palace or a bustling market, you could probably say the same in similar circumstances of any spot on England's rural/urban fringe. To see Draycott at its other extreme, and to get a flavour of the place, come with me on a balmy summer evening to indulge in that most English of pastimes: a local pub crawl. To keep our senses sharp, I suggest just half a pint at each inn!

Let's start the tour from the eastern end of the village, on the crest of the railway bridge, looking down towards Draycott. As many will recall, a glance to the left would once have given a view over the local railway station, sadly gone for over thirty years now, but here's another mystery already: though the station was actually in Breaston, when it opened in 1852 it was called 'Draycott' – why? (History Mystery 2)

Descending the bridge, and passing some rather grand houses on the left with rear views down to the Derwent, we see against the towering

Draycott Mills, first developed by local industrialist John Towle in 1814. Just before we re-enter civilisation, in the form of Derby Road, we pass through a public area comprising an odd jumble of huts; odder still when you notice that they each form the home for a different local group: the cadets, the scouts, the youth club, the senior citizens etc. In fact, at the time of writing, the local Parish Council is busy investigating the possibility of replacing them all with a single community centre – a proposal, though no doubt eminently reasonable to an outsider, that has raised more local hackles than on a hound on heat!

And so we come to **The Traveller's Rest**, located as you will have noticed in a local 'Apostrophe Triangle', where many apostrophes disappear without trace, only to emerge again in quite the wrong place. As 'Travellers Rest', perhaps it's just a simple statement – that's what travellers do – or even an instruction, missing only its exclamation mark. Punctuational barbs aside, the ale is good and the bar-side banter probably the liveliest in the village. This is the second pub building on this site, the old inn of the same name having been replaced in 1897. Today's landlord is Peter Lawson and, with its three rooms, its open fire in winter, its Irish music session on St Patrick's Day and its huddle of locals at the bar all year round, this is perhaps the Draycott pub to have best retained its traditional character... except of course for the ubiquitous satellite TV.

And so we amble cheerily back along the main road to our final pub, studiously avoiding the old factory's olfactory temptations... no, I tell a lie, it's the smell from the fish and chip shop across the road. On the way, we pass the old Draycott Council School, now Draycott Primary School, opened in 1905 as a bigger replacement for the National School, which used to stand on the eastern corner of The Square, on what was then called The Green, a name now used, oddly enough, for the area on the opposite side of the road... near where we now notice another missing apostrophe! And just to confuse matters further, why does Draycott have a Market Street when no-one seems to be able to remember a market? (History Mystery 7).

Passing the former butcher's shop of Mr Fritchley (the house with the cast-iron verandah) and two legacies of late 20th-century England – the Chinese takeaway and the charity shop – we come to **The Victoria**.

Still sometimes known as The Victoria Hotel and locally known as 'The Middle House', this pub appears in many an early photograph of the village, architecturally in much the same shape as today. Talking with current managers Marie and John Green and their regulars, we learn that the lounge bar on the left used to be a butcher's shop and that the pub's original name is believed to have been The Axe & Cleaver; if so, the name change would doubtless have removed some confusion with the old Cleaver's Inn on South Street.

So now we've completed our tour of the village, let's focus on the final mystery. Did you notice one thing missing? What about that typical ingredient of an English village: the old parish church? Well, if you look out of The Victoria's front window, you'll see Draycott's parish church across the road: St Mary's. Hm, where's the spire, the graveyard, the little porch and all the other ingredients you might expect? In fact, this 1830 building wasn't even built as an Anglican church, but as another Wesleyan chapel. However, we know from our saunter around the back streets that the village was an old agricultural community from at least the 1600s (in fact, from much earlier)... so where's the original parish church? (History Mystery 8)

Anyway, I hope this pub crawl has convinced you that there's a little more to Draycott than a few shops on the busy road between Long Eaton and Derby. We've seen old farms, gentleman's lodges, coaching inns and Victorian mills... as well as modern housing of all types. In fact, in a 1984 article, Derbyshire historian Roy Christian called Draycott "an unexpected sandwich of a place"[1]. What a good idea! Cheese and pickle for me, I think. What can I tempt you with?

of Wilne Toll Bridge, sited just downstream from the current aqueduct. The oldest known structure here was a wooden bridge which carried light traffic, including the horses of the Harrington Hunt, until it collapsed in 1936. Connecting an unsurfaced track from Great Wilne and Shardlow to what was a continuation of the public road to Church Wilne and Draycott (now within the private land of the firework factory), Wilne Bridge formed part of the regular journey to work for many of the workers at Draycott, paying their penny toll to the Wilmots at the toll house, and for Wilne Mill employees, who were exempted from the toll. In fact, for a short period after the closure of the Derby Canal, coal carts also came this way to Draycott from Shardlow Wharf and one wonders if this relatively heavy traffic contributed to the bridge's demise. After the collapse, a pedestrian-only bridge was built and opened in 1937. This later structure, now a rusty hulk that still spans the river, was closed to public access by Haley and Weller in 1950 (despite vehement protests from both sides of the river, and the old toll house also still stands as the two-storey building on the northern (private) bank, but still visible from the south. A river crossing was finally reinstated many years later with the modern footbridge, 250 metres downstream, shortening the route for some between Great Wilne and Church Wilne by 12 miles!

In fact, one of the ferries mentioned above was a temporary affair specifically for the 'south bank' employees of Wilne Mills in the bridgeless years 1936-37, although this was on the site of a former ferry in use at least at the time of the Civil War. The other was one that many local people will remember as the Ambaston Ferry or the chain ferry. This vessel, not much bigger than a regular rowing boat and guided across the channel by a fixed chain, ran between The Ferry House in Draycott (the house lying straight on where Wilne Road bends left) and the right bank, from where an overgrown footpath still veers westward to Ambaston. The fare in the 1930s for this service was one penny. Its origins are unknown and there is some debate about its demise. Local memory favours the idea that it was still in operation until the 1950s and that the service stopped only when the ferryboat was stolen and taken downriver, never to be seen in Draycott again. The parish records, however, note that it was withdrawn from service by the Air Ministry during the Second World War for security purposes (had German paratroopers landed in Ambaston?!) and, despite council enquiries in

1951, there is no official record of the ferry's reinstatement.

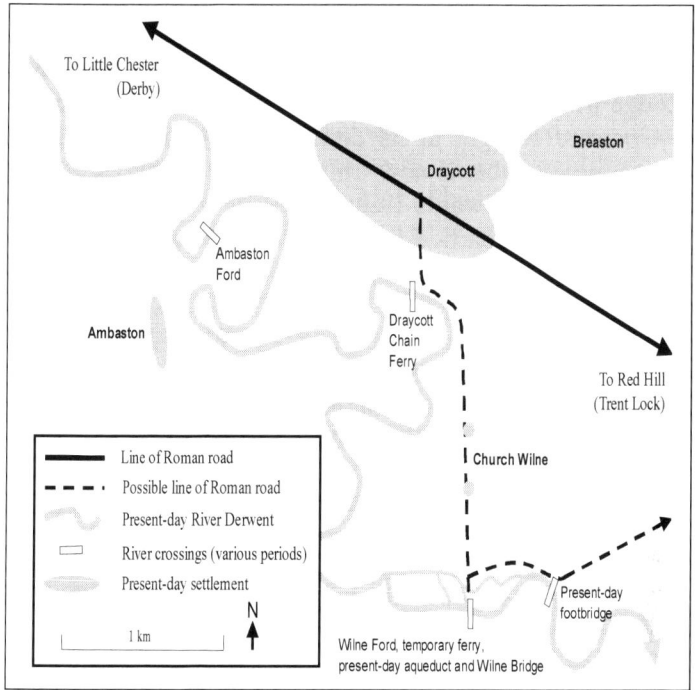

Roman roads and Derwent river crossings

All roads lead to... lead

Given all that we've just said about the Derwent, it's ironic that the earliest artifact still visible in the area today derived from the location of another river and another crossing point. The principle function of the major Roman roads in Britain was military: to enable the swift movement of troops around the colony. However, the short Roman road whose route now forms Draycott's Derby Road – Victoria Road – Sawley Road axis is reputed to have had another significant purpose: the transport of lead ore by pack mule from Derbyshire's mines. This ore, from which silver could be extracted, was first brought to Little Chester (Derby's Roman precursor, just north of the present-day city) and from there through what is now Chaddesden, Spondon, Borrowash, Draycott and Sawley to the

the clue to the mystery of the missing Wilne. Although the mill was referred to as Sawley Mill, it's almost certain that this was at Wilne; likewise, the two churches must have been those at Sawley and Wilne. So, the only conclusion to draw is that the name of Wilne was simply omitted by mistake – one of many errors known to exist in the Domesday Book.

A village by any other name...

Over the years, the spelling of Draycott variously appears as *Draicot* (1086), *Draicote*, *Dreycote* (1259), *Dracot* (1502) and *Draycott*. The name probably means 'cottage at or near a portage', from the Old English *draeg*, meaning, as we have mentioned, to drag or draw; or possibly 'shed where the drays were kept'.

Draycott's variations are easily outdone by Church Wilne's. It has variously appeared as *Wilne, Wilna, Wylne, Wylna, Wille, Wilene, Wilen, Wylene, Kyrke Wyllne, Lytle Wylney, Little Welne, Little Wilne* and *Church Wilne*. The name Wilne is Anglo-Saxon and means 'willow copse'. Though 'Church Wilne' is a relatively recent title, I use it throughout this book to avoid confusion – and simply to distinguish it from the settlement of Great Wilne across the water.

Chain ferry, from the Ambaston bank, date unknown
Photo: Long Eaton Library

Harringtons! It was the 11th Earl who left Elvaston for Ireland in the 1930s and eventually sold the estate in 1963 to meet the expense of death duties.

Derbyshire County Council and Derby Corporation jointly bought it in 1969 and developed the estate into Elvaston Country Park.

The ownership of the *prebendal* manor of Sawley, which we know from the details of one of the sales included at least some land in Draycott, had a more chequered history. First, in 1450 the Bishop of Lichfield granted the lease to his brother Roger Booth – we can only wonder how this use of the church's resources was explained away! On expiry of the Booths' lease in 1550, the prebendary manor passed to Geoffrey Edmundson and then in 1627 to Sir Edward Leech of Shipley. The Holden family of Aston-on-Trent bought it in 1732, when it was noted that both St Chad's church and some tithe barns in Draycott were in good repair. (A 'tithe barn' was for storage of agricultural produce delivered in lieu of the tax or 'tithe' due to the lord of the manor, theoretically for the upkeep of the church; one of these barns stood near the south-east corner of the junction between Market Street and what is now Victoria Road.) Finally, in 1808 the prebendary himself, Rev. Spencer Madan, took over the prebendary manor and eventually managed to convert the leasehold rights into freehold – quite how is unknown!

The mill on the island

One of the prize assets in the manor of Sawley – and it fell within the non-prebendary manor – was Wilne Mills. Where the river flows west-to-east between Church Wilne and Great Wilne, a weir forms a barrier to the to the stream's smooth flow and just upstream from this a portion of its flow has been diverted through the north (Church Wilne) bank along an artificial channel parallel to the main stream. The natural flow of this channel back towards the river, now at a lower level, could then be controlled by sluices and the force of the water harnessed for power and applied in a mill. Who originally built a mill here and when is unknown, but as we've seen one was already in place in 1086. The artificial channel, or mill race, created an island in the river about 750 metres long by 100 metres wide, divided into three islets by two short, north-south channels between the parallel courses of the river, each with a sluice gate at its head. (At one time eels were caught between the sluice gates and specially-shaped eel traps below them, and salmon were seen attempting to swim up the weir; indeed we learn that in later years the mills' workers – and customers – were granted special fishing rights in the vicinity of Wilne Mills.) The location of the outlet from the larger of these two sluices can still be seen from the south bank of the river, as a collection of large bushes just to the west of the the aqueduct and old bridge crossing the river. The line of the old mill stream can also still be distinguished from Wilne Road, as the line of trees beyond the field that lies between the current factory entrance and the point where the road runs beside the river.

It's almost certain that the early use of the mill's water power was to grind corn, since this would have been a vital requirement to the farming community and indeed old millstones have been found to form part of the sluice material. There are several local tales of the earliest millers being a community of monks and moreover that the mill was connected to St Chad's by a secret tunnel. Given the height of the local water table, the latter is less likely to be true than the former. By 1536, according to an entry in Jeayes' *Derbyshire Charters*, 'Wylne myll' was used for fulling, i.e. cleaning fleeces of wool by immersing them in a mixture of water and fuller's earth and then beating them with hammers. In 1634 it's recorded that the then lord of the manor, Henry Stanhope, spent £75 repairing his mills and a house at Wilne (unfortunately a precursor of more serious repairs to come). It had been 'mill*s*' plural for some time, and a survey of 1651 gives us the number, in referring to "all those six water mill under one roofe... whereof four are cloth mills or wake [fulling] mills and two grist [corn grinding] mills"[6]

By the early 18th century Wilne Mills were used for rolling and slitting lead, but by 1781 the mills' main activity had been switched to the new boom industry of 18th-century Britain, one that was to be in the vanguard of the new factory system at the heart of the industrial revolution: cotton. This enterprise was founded by Stretton, Thacker and Co., the Thackers already having been involved in the lead-based activities, and Wilne cotton mill was only the second in England, after Arkwright and Strutt's mill at Cromford. The new business must have been an instant success, for Pilkington's 1789 *View of Derbyshire* quotes Wilne cotton mill as being the principal means of support for the inhabitants of the district of Sawley. The workers would have brought some existing skills since for many years cotton yarn had been spun and cloth woven locally as a 'cottage industry' in people's own homes. We'll resume the story of Wilne Mills and the local textile industry in the next chapter.

As all about them lost their heads...

Two violent periods in the 16th century had indirect connections with Draycott and Church Wilne. By the 1530s, the Christian church in Europe had split between Roman Catholicism and Protestantism (in it various guises). In the 1550s, persecution of Protestants was rife in England under the Catholic Mary Tudor ('Bloody Mary') and at the Windmill Pit in Derby a blind young Protestant woman called Joan Waste was executed after a certain Doctor Draicot had publicly denounced her physical blindness as a reflection of her religious blindness. Whether Doctor Draicot actually came from 'Draicot' is unknown.

Thirty years later the Protestants were at it! One of the victims of Catholic persecution under the Protestant Elizabeth I was a native of Wilne, one William Hartley. He began distributing Catholic propaganda in 1580, twice left England for France (once voluntarily and once deported) and was found guilty of plotting to depose the Queen. Hartley was eventually executed at Shoreditch (London) in 1588.

Religious rivalries were also among the underlying causes of the Civil War sixty years later, although again Draycott and Church Wilne are not known to have been directly involved in any large-scale skirmishes. The Stanhopes, by then lords of the manor but not yet Earls of Harrington, were Royalists, while Derby was a Roundhead headquarters under Sir John Gell. During the course of the war, Gell took Wilne Ferry and Swarkestone Bridge from the Royalists. With the Roundhead victory, the Stanhopes' properties were confiscated and in 1650 the manor of Sawley was taken up by John Pymme of Draycott... only to have it returned to the Stanhopes in 1656.

A happier time was had in Draycott in 1760 with a local celebration of George III's coronation day. It was reported thus in the Derby Mercury: "The Loyal Inhabitants of the small village of Draycote in this County greatly signalized themselves in honouring the day ... a grand procession round the Town, amidst some hundreds of spectators ... A booth was built in the middle of the Town to dine near 200 people .. the Healths of King George III and Queen Charlotte went round with the greatest Acclamations of Joy."[7]

... or was it just the free booze?! The 200 diners were doubtless formed from the village's social elite, since the report later mentions that "the Remains of the Provisions ... was (sic) immediately given to the Poor of the Town."

And Parliament said: let there be hedges

Four years later, in 1764, an event of rather more significance to the villages of Draycott and Church Wilne took place. For a number of years, increasing population and technical developments in agriculture had been putting pressure on the country's farming industry to improve efficiency, and the major obstacle to this was seen by many to be the open field system still prevalent in most areas at the time, including this part of the Midlands. The medieval system of open fields divided into strips or 'lands' created the ridge-and-furrow pattern still visible in the fields off Wilne Road. The lands were allocated to different farmers whose holdings therefore comprised portions distributed inconveniently around the village. For example, in the will of Thomas Brown in the 1740s, he left his wife those lands "lying and being in two certain fields in Draycott, namely two lands in ye Tinkley field and one land in ye Burrow field."[8] Although each field was usually devoted to just one crop – in this area wheat, barley (for brewing), oats (for horses), rye or peas, for example – this wasn't always the case. All in all the system, though fair, was rather inefficient.

The response to the pressure for higher productivity was the enclosure movement, an unstoppable coalition of social, economic and political leaders in favour of 'enclosing' the existing open fields, i.e. selling them off to individual farmers who could then physically enclose them, possibly after combining a number of fields, to devote each field to one crop and enable the use of newly developed machinery and other techniques. The enclosure of land in this area was covered by the 1764 Enclosure Act, which approved the enclosure of 75% of the land in Draycott, with the largest allocation being to – yes, you guessed it – the Earl of Harrington. In fact, it was an entirely predictable trend across the country that the only people who could afford to buy up most of the rights were those who were already the largest landholders, while at the other extreme, those who had worked the smallest smallholdings were the ones evicted. Farms were consolidated and many who had previously worked land that they rented themselves became employees of the new 'farmer', often a farmer in name only, there being many absentee landlords.

Whatever the social and economic consequences of enclosure, its impact on the English landscape was permanent, leading to larger fields with single crops, and, since the physical erection of boundaries was usually a legal responsibility of the new landowner, the relatively sudden emergence of mile-on-mile of hedgerows.

A mania hits Draycott

Around the same time, a revolution was also afoot in the country's transport system. The poor condition of Britain's roads and the restricted and unpredictable access to inland areas offered by navigable rivers, were threatening to put a brake on economic development. While the expansion of turnpike trusts addressed the roadway problems, water-borne transport received a boost in 1761 with the opening of Britain's first man-made canal, the Duke of Bridgwater's Worsley Canal near Manchester. This was an immediate success and further schemes followed, including the Trent and Mersey (Grand Trunk) and Erewash Canals. The 1790s saw the peak of canal-building and it is during this decade of 'canal mania' that the Derby Canal was cut through Draycott.

The Derby Canal was authorised in 1793 and opened in 1796, the engineer being Benjamin Outram. It had an unusual geographical alignment, being an inverted V-shape with its northern apex being in Derby, linked by the canal's south-western arm to the Trent and Mersey Canal at Swarkestone and by its eastern arm to the Erewash Canal at Sandiacre. Very little business was accounted for by through traffic, most being to or from Derby itself. Like most canals at the time, its primary business was coal and this would have constituted the major east-west traffic through Draycott, from the coalfields of the Erewash Valley and beyond. Although a basin was cut in the canal alongside the canal bridge on Hopwell Road, coal for the village was offloaded at a wharf opposite Nooning Lane (then called Wharf Lane) and brought by horse-drawn cart along Derby Road. This must have only served to emphasise Draycott's local nickname of 'Neddytown', which is reputed to have derived originally from its position as a changing point for the coal-cart donkeys from the north before the canal took over the trade.

Draycott takes shape

Despite the rumblings of industrialisation towards the end of the 18th century, in the form of the cotton mill and the canal, Draycott and Church Wilne were still essentially agricultural villages, albeit growing ones: the 1801 census gave the combined population as 690, this being bigger than either Long Eaton or Breaston, though smaller than Sawley.

The current street layout of central Draycott was already in place by then, a mid-18th century map showing development along South Street (the old main street, possibly called Town Street at the time), Lodge Street, the present Victoria Road, Market Street and Wilne Road. In the triangle between what is now Station Road and Sawley Road was to be found the village 'pinfold', where all stray cattle were impounded – by the officially-designated 'impounder'.

The village's buildings already included some that we still see today:

- The **tall barn on South St** (now Beetroot Tree Gallery) is thought to have been built in the early 17th century and therefore probably the oldest surviving building in Draycott.
- The **Manor House**, part of the former Manor Farm at the junction of Lodge Street and South Street, includes a 17th-century gable. This house carries with it a couple of legends: that a rumoured tunnel (purpose unknown) between Draycott and Church Wilne used to have its entrance here and that a ghost (identity hitherto unknown) still haunts the property. However, research for this book seems to have revealed the identity of the Manor House 'ghost'! Raymond Coulson revealed to the author that he and his pals used to indulge in a little night-time 'spirit-tapping' in their youth. This involved attaching a suitably weighted nut part way along a length of black cotton and then securing one end of the cotton to a window frame and the other to the ground. Taking up the slack pulled the line so taut that just a little flick here and there would have the nut rhythmically tapping at the window like… well, like a ghost. Mr Coulson confirms that the Manor House was one of their 'haunts' and that the subsequent female

screams were very satisfactory indeed!
- In the late 18th century, **Cedars Farmhouse** was built. Grade-II-listed since 1979, this is the unnamed farm beyond the southern junction of Market Street and South Street.
- 1795 saw the construction of Draycott's first non-conformist chapel: the **Wesleyan Chapel** on Lodge Street, now Chapel House.
- Off the southern end of Lodge Street stands **Draycott Lodge** which some claim to have been built originally in 1675 (a Cedar of Lebanon planted in its garden soon after is still there) and then extended during the 18th century. However, a recent survey[9] for the Derby Buildings Record dates the core of the current building at around 1800, with major improvements around 1830. This survey classifies it as a 'gentleman's house', especially given the name 'Lodge' which was typically used in the period for the residence of a 'gentleman', in the sense of a class of minor nobility. In 1842 it was noted as including a coach house and stables, as well as farm buildings.
- **Draycott Hall**, on Derwent Street, was actually built during the early 19th century but is believed to incorporate part of an earlier building, as well as later Victorian additions. It used to incorporate something intriguingly defined as a 'pleasure ground' and its gardens stretched over land now occupied by the houses on the north side of Derwent Street. The feature most visible from the surrounding streets and gardens today, however, is the timber dovecote surmounting the block to the rear of the hall, formerly comprising a coach house and stables. Draycott Hall's earliest known owner was Joseph Bourne and it has been listed (Grade II) since 1986.
- Some way out of the village, to the west of Hopwell Road, **Draycott House** was built in the late 18th century. This three-storey edifice was designed by Joseph Pickford of Derby and bears a close resemblance to his design for John Howitt's house (now The Hall) in Long Eaton. 'The

Cottage', immediately to the north-west of Draycott House, is also 18th-century and was originally the stable block and coach house.

A similar roll-call cannot be made for Church Wilne, of course, since of the 18th-century village only the church itself now remains! We left the story of St Chad's with the wooden Anglo-Saxon church at the time of the Domesday. The current structure was built in the 14th and 15th centuries, probably as a rebuilding of an earlier Norman structure, since traces of an earlier (13th-century?) design remain, for example the ridge line of an earlier roof on the east face of the tower. In 1622-4, the south aisle was extended to form the mortuary chapel of the Willoughby family, lords of the manor of Risley since the 14th century. St Chad's is the parish's only Grade-I listed building (since 1967) and readers interested in a more detailed architectural survey are referred to the Church History by the Friends of St Chad's (see bibliography).

Even when some of its flock lived in the village of Church Wilne itself, many of St Chad's parishioners faced a very long haul to the church, since up to 1719 its parochial rights – for baptisms, weddings and burials – took in not only Draycott, but also Breaston, Risley and Hopwell. The 'Coffin Walk' from Breaston to Wilne is still a public right of way and one of the large stones provided for coffin-bearers to rest their load on has been preserved *en route*. The regular long walk seems to have been a particular challenge to one parson, whose sad tale is told below.

Drunk in charge of the parish?

Thomas Humphries was appointed as parson at St Chad's in 1785. Around 1811, a case was brought against him in the court of the Dean and Chapter of Lichfield by four local parishioners: Messrs. Eaton, Raynor, Thacker and Hewitt. The charges include leaving corpses unburied in the church overnight; refusing without reason to marry Joseph Clifford and Mary Smedley; leaving a service to feed his chickens; stealing his neighbour's chickens; failing to turn up for services; frequently turning up for services with a black eye; being so drunk at the Shakespeare in Derby as to be incapable of mounting his horse for the return journey; also being drunk in Draycott and at John Clifford's alehouse in Long Eaton; getting into a fight with a stranger in the same alehouse; and finally attacking the church bellringers on New Year's Eve 1803 whilst expressing in foul language his displeasure at the noise.

The Rev. Humphries had a ready excuse for every charge, including failure to hear the bells calling him to church; encountering difficulties in reaching Church Wilne through inclement weather, including rain, snow and treacherous floods; falling into the Derwent from a cart that had been sent to fetch him; and even, when finally arriving, finding not a soul in the congregation. Whatever the truth of these extraneous circumstances, they certainly bring home to us the effective remoteness of even physically close local villages before the surfacing of minor roads. No conclusion was reached on any of the charges, but Humphries was eventually replaced by a parson of more traditional comportment in 1815.

The strange case of the flying corpse

The simple business of burials seems to have been the source of one problem after another in these parts. In the 1930s a certain school governor and some-time undertaker's assisant, who should perhaps remain nameless but was a short, dignified gentleman with a sharply sculpted goatee beard, was one day taking his accustomed place at the front-right corner of a coffin as it was carefully manoeuvred down a flight of stairs. The combination of the steep stair and the coffin-bearer's short stature unfortunately presented too tempting an angle to the coffin's occupant, who, to the consternation of onlooking relatives, emerged from his supposedly last resting place at some speed, dealing our bearded friend a severe blow en route to the bottom of the stairs, where he was rapidly joined by the latter, complete with broken leg!

The ghost in the graveyard

Another ghost story that has done the rounds of the village is the account of a Saturday-night drinker returning a little unsteadily to Church Wilne, where he reported seeing a hooded figure rise up from the graveyard, prompting him to race on to Wilne toll gate shouting "Gate! Gate!", in order to hasten his escape.

This mystery too has been cleared up by Raymond Coulson, who identfies the 'hooded figure' as the old church stoker, attending to the fire which used to stand at the north side of the church, warming the building for Sunday morning's service. And on a cold winter's night, who wouldn't drape an old blanket around their head to keep warm and dry in a dank old graveyard?

4. Industrial Outposts (1800 – 1907)

Cotton Towle

The industrial 'rumblings' took a significant step in 1800, when John Towle, destined to be a big noise in Draycott, started a cotton doubling business in the village (exactly where we don't know). Business must have boomed, for in 1814 Towle constructed the first buildings at the **Draycott Mills** site (on the west side of Market Street), a location that was to witness a bewildering variety of commercial activities, right up to the 21st century. Towle expanded his mill only four years later and it was probably around this time that Coulson's Yard and Coxon's Yard were built. These were short terraces at right-angles to Market Street, to the south of the mill, on land now occupied by Milner Avenue. In 1842 the present Draycott Mills buildings were started, including Draycott Lace Mill (also known as Melbourne Mill), the long and now rather dilapidated section that fronts on to Market Street (a Grade-II listed building since 1986). The octagonal chimney to the rear of the site, and which still stands as Draycott's second-highest landmark, was completed in 1860, as recorded by the plaque halfway up its eastern side. At around the same time, more housing was built for the workers, on Clay Street and New Street.

Lace manufacturing had in fact made its first appearance in Draycott in 1842, probably at another mill owned by the Towle family and situated by the canal a little way east of Draycott Fields Farm, using cotton yarn from Manchester and elsewhere.

So the leading entrepreneur in this phase of Draycott's industrial development was undoubtedly John Towle and when he died in 1861, by the terms of his will a bible was given to each of the 323 employees of Draycott Mill, an event which, according to the Derby Mercury caused "a considerable degree of excitement"[10].

Wilne Mills were still going strong at this time, with cotton spinning and doubling, their employment peaking at 190 people in 1871 when Marcus Astle was the owner, but the new businesses were all being set up away from the flood plain in Draycott. 1895 saw the construction of another lace factory, this time on Derby Road by Joseph and Arthur

Bryan, their premises now having been converted into the Conservative Club, and in the same year Draycott Mills was host to the Fairbank Wood Rim Company (wooden bike wheel rims) and Simpson's Lever Chain and Cycle Company. However, all these developments were eclipsed by the mammoth enterprise whose construction lasted from 1888 to 1907 and which gave Draycott its dominant landmark to this day.

So how big was Noah's Ark anyway?

It's long and tall, it's bright green on top and you can see it for miles around: it's **Victoria Mills**, Draycott. Its Listed Building Record Card (Grade II since 1986) claims it is "reputedly the largest lace factory in the world"[11]. I'm not going to argue. Even given its vast scale, 19 years still seems rather an excessive time to complete a single factory, and indeed the history of its construction forms a rather more interesting tale than the history of its use since completion.

First things first. When the Rev. Madan's heirs sold his Draycott property in the 1860s, not quite all of it went to the Harringtons: a field called Nether Town End Close, between Station Road and the railway, was acquired by Joseph Bosworth, who later sold it to Ernest Terah Hooley. Now, Hooley was indeed something of a 'terror' in the local business world, apparently addicted to the speculative purchase and subsequent sale of land not only in the Long Eaton area but also elsewhere in England… until he was declared bankrupt in 1898.

In 1887, Hooley sold a share of Nether Town Close to one Henry Cooper (I am not making this up), the two of them filing a plan for the development of the area with a mill, confusingly called 'Draycott Mills'. It was to have an Italianate frontage with a clock tower topped by a cupola, a popular design at the time, also used in Long Eaton Co-operative Society's new Central Stores built in the same period[*]. Cooper and Hooley's plan also included streets for housing, including Town End Road, Elvaston Street and Derwent Street (now Villa Street). At the time, there was very little development at this eastern end of the village, there being just five houses on the north side of Station Road. Construction started on the central section of the mill in 1888 and the following year Hooley sold his part of the property to Cooper, who therefore became the

---

[*] Draycott's example has survived in rather better repair than Long Eaton's.

sole owner and the mill became known as 'Cooper's Factory'.

Hooley wasn't out of things for long though, because in 1893 he bought some land to the south-east of Town End Road from Cooper, quickly selling it on for house-building. In 1896, with the mill still under construction, Cooper sold it to Benjamin Horton of Birmingham, who sold it two months later to... Terah Hooley! The following year, Hooley leased it to Edward Cope & Co of Nottingham, whose directors were Ernest Jardine and... Henry Cooper! (I hope you're still following this!) In 1898, the northern section was completed, just in time for Hooley to go bankrupt. Jardine bought the property from the receiver, bringing some much-needed stability, since he was to retain ownership until 1946. By 1902, 'Jardine's Mill' was finally nearing completion, with much of the new southern section under construction... but disaster was soon to strike.

On Saturday 17th January 1902, a fire broke out in the southernmost block and the Long Eaton Fire Brigade was called out. Soon after their arrival it became clear that the fire was well beyond the capacity of their manual pumping gear and the Nottingham Brigade was called out to assist. Though they pulled out all the stops to get to the scene on time (ten miles in 45 minutes), they too found their manual equipment to be inadequate and the assistance of the Derby Brigade was requested by 'telegraphic message'. 16 firemen and a steam fire engine arrived from Derby and hoses were rapidly laid to the Derwent, three fields away. Alas, it was all too late: the southern block was by now beyond rescue, although a fireproof wall did save the rest of the factory. The cost of the inferno: 50 lace machines lost; £30,000 damage (covered by insurance); and 150 of the 500 mill workers temporarily out of a job (not covered by insurance).

The burnt-out block was rebuilt by 1904 and, undaunted by the accident, Jardine had two new blocks built as well. The tower was completed in 1906, as recorded on the street side of the tower. Subsequent painting of the clock face seems to have been another hazardous activity, with no sign of hard hats – but Raymond Coulson, who remembers undertaking the job, dismisses the danger. "I painted it standing on a suspended plank that was only 1¼ inches thick", recalls Mr Coulson. "With my weight, it bent further and further in the middle until I couldn't reach the the 12 o'clock position. So I balanced a stool on the plank and perched on that. Mind you, after our tea break, I thought it was a good idea to tie a rope around my waist, just in case."

By 1907 the whole factory was completed and the official opening ceremony, on September 17th of that year, was evidently a day to remember for the villagers of Draycott. Everyone assembled in the Market Place and, preceded by a band under the baton of Mr Pounder, marched to 'Victoria Mills', now its official name, after the Queen's golden jubilee in 1887, the year construction had started. Here, appropriately to the strains of the Rule Britannia and the National Anthem, Mrs Jardine formally started the clock which, then as now, peers majestically over the village beneath, its green cupola above and (now only on the Station Street side) Jardine's name below. The time, we are told, was 1:59 p.m. All the children then set off for Mr Beresford's field for a grand session of games and sports, prizes being donated by Mr Jardine. In fact, Jardine financed the whole day, providing tea for 800 at the factory, some 'cinematograph entertainment' and a newly opened Post Office bank account for each Draycott child, with an opening balance of one shilling. His words in addressing the assembled crowd are worth recording: "I shall pass through the world but once; therefore any good thing that I do or any kindness I may show, let me do it now; let me not neglect it; I shall not pass this way again."[12]

Despite Jardine's confidence, the lace trade fell into decline after the First World War and standings became vacant from the 1920s onwards. Gradually tenants from other trades began to take up the standings, including manufacturers of hosiery and woollens and the first electrical engineers. W. J. Parry and Sons worked in this latter trade and bought the mill from the Jardine Company in 1957, prompting a fifth name for the building: 'Parry's Mill'*. The 1960s saw a further decline in the lace trade and while over half of the mill's workers had still been laceworkers in 1953, the last lace manufacturer left in 1970.

A few facts about Victoria Mills

- It was built as a 'tenement mill', i.e. its occupants were small lace manufacturers with only a few machines,

---

* The five are: Draycott Mills, Cooper's Factory, Jardine's Mills, Victoria Mills and Parry's Mill.

possibly only one, each.
- The physical layout was standard for lace mills at the time, being divided into 'standings', each occupied by one lace machine and in this case running east to west across the factory. The narrow building and large windows (228 down one side) meant that daylight was widely available.
- Each tenant rented both space and machine from the owner, Ernest Jardine, who manufactured lace machines.
- Power was originally supplied by two on-site steam engines; one engine ceased operation only in 1959, when it was under the care of the engineer, Mr Haywood.
- Until 1952 there were no toilets in the building and much time was spent scrambling up and down the four flights of stairs to use the outdoor facilities[*].
- The factory is often quoted as being 'as big as Noah's Ark'. To modern minds this seems a strange comparison, Noah's Ark usually being represented as dwarfed by the necks of two cartoon giraffes protruding from within! However, the Bible says the dimensions of the craft were 300 cubits (150m) long by 50 cubits (25m) wide by 30 cubits (15m) high. The approximate dimensions of Victoria Mills are 295m long by 15m wide by 25m high (to the top of the cupola), and so the comparison is in any case an underestimate... not to mention the dubious seaworthiness of any craft shaped like Victoria Mills! Using a more modern yardstick, the factory is over twice the length of the largest official football pitch, but only a third the width of the smallest, while its height is not particularly unusual for lace mills. What *are* remarkable are its narrow shape, the body being even narrower than the façade, and its massive proportions relative to the village that spreads at it feet.

---

[*] Strangely enough, the vexed question of lavatorial provision crops up again more than once in the unfolding tale of Draycott.

Tiny Town

| Total Population from Census Returns ||||
Census Year	Draycott + Church Wilne	Draycott (alone)	Church Wilne (alone)
1801	690	n/a	n/a
1811	892	n/a	n/a
1821	1102	n/a	n/a
1831	1074	n/a	n/a
1841	1118	895	223
1851	1161	987	174
1861	1156	1016	140
1871	1028	896	132
1881	1015	n/a	n/a
1891	1032	n/a	n/a
1901	1504	n/a	n/a
1911	2218	n/a	n/a
1921	2454	2364	90
1931	2339	n/a	n/a
1951	2227	2197	30
1961	1995	n/a	n/a
1971	2200	n/a	n/a
1981	2798	n/a	n/a
1991	2782	2777	5

It's not surprising that the industrial developments culminating in the Victoria Mills enterprise contributed to a rising population for Draycott and Church Wilne parish, as demonstrated by the census returns shown above.

Church Wilne's share, however, was falling, with its 38 houses in 1845 (compared with 226 in Draycott) shrinking to 30 in 1866 (Draycott 460) and only 14 in 1895. In fact, for most of the 19th century, a larger community lived in Wilne Mills than in the village itself, including the mill-owner's family, who occupied a large house built over the stream, giving them the unusual facility of being able to fish directly from the lounge window! However, all the bits and pieces of a growing village's infrastructure arrived in the environs of Draycott, rather than of its ailing neighbour down the lane.

Draycott got its **railway station** in 1852, towards the end of the first period of 'railway mania' in Britain, which had already eclipsed the 'canal mania' of fifty years before in both extent and impact. The Midland Counties Railway had opened its Nottingham-Derby line on 30th May 1839, when, amidst widespread excitement and celebration four first-class and two second-class carriages were hauled from Nottingham to Derby by the steam engine *Sunbeam*, to be followed by an even larger train hauled by *Ariel*, covering the 15 miles in 44 minutes at a fantastic 21 mph. The line's route through Draycott was mostly in a cutting, an alignment which today creates the odd situation where a passing train creates less noise the closer you are to the railway! Still spanning the cutting stand two original 1839 road bridges (Hopwell Road and Town End Road), designed by the Midland Counties' engineer C B Vignoles and, since 1986, registered as listed 'buildings' (Grade II). However, the village didn't get its own station until after the company had built its extensions to Leicester and then Rugby, whence connection could be made with the London and Birmingham company's line to Euston. The station was built just over the parish boundary in Breaston, which village it also served, but was initially named simply 'Draycott' so as to avoid confusion with Beeston. The main station buildings were on the north (London/Nottingham-bound) side, from where access to the south (Derby-bound) side was by an iron footbridge. There was also a wooden-sleeper crossing at track level for use by railway personnel. It was here that a tragedy occurred on 12th March 1904, when on a foggy day the stationmaster John Stanford was struck by a train and killed. His grave in Hopwell Road cemetary is marked by a fine headstone erected by voluntary contributions from villagers.

In 1857 there were seven trains a day from Draycott to Derby and six to Nottingham (change at Trent for Leicester and London). It finally became 'Draycott & Breaston' station in 1939 and closed in 1966 due to loss of passenger traffic to bus services. Nowadays, alas, you wouldn't know there had ever been a station there at all.

Despite the railway's arrival in the mid-19th century, carrier's carts were still used to transport goods to and from Derby and Nottingham. The starting place was a yard at the junction of Market Street and South Street and carriers included Thomas Astle (mentioned in 1857), Henry Johnson (1876 and 1888) and Robert Springthorpe (1888). Carts left for Derby on Fridays and Nottingham on Wednesdays and Saturdays.

A Victorian Snapshot

One of the reasons that these sorts of historical details suddenly become available to us from the 19th century is the Victorians' obsession with the listing and classification of everything that moved – and of plenty of things that didn't, for that matter. *Slater's (National) Directory* of 1862 gives us a detailed snapshot of the business activity in Draycott and Church Wilne – detailed, but unfortunately not particularly comprehensive, and so the table below includes some additions based on information from other sources, notably the 1842 Parish Valuation, reported by Burrows[13]. With that caveat, here is Slater's list of local businesses, all but Tillard & Co in fact being in Draycott:

Businesses in Draycott and Church Wilne, 1862		
Category	Business	Name
Industry	Textiles	Tillard & Co
		John Towle & Co
		[Unnamed]
Shops	Grocer/draper	George Astle
		Peter Battelle
		Thomas Coxon

	Butcher	Zadoch Hill
		Smith & Son
	Beer retailer	Stephen Walker
	Baker	Samuel Moore
	Cobbler	Samuel Astle
		William Astle
		Charles Gregory
		Henry Taylor
	'General'	Joseph Bosworth
	Post office	John Gregory
	Tailor	Ralph Gamble
		Henry Plackett
	Chemist	William Salmon Charlton
Catering	Pub	Victoria Hotel (James Cupit)
		Coach & Horses (Wm Wignall)
		Rose & Crown (Joseph Gill)
Other services	Blacksmith	Robert Chollerton
		William Chollerton*
	Bricklayer	John Elson
	Ferryman	Probably Mr Sherwin
	Framesmith	Richard Slater
	Joiner	George Daft
		William Daft
		Robert Theobald
	Plumber	Edward Clay
		John Clifford
	Ropemaker	Richard Elliot
	Seedsman/ gardener	George Astle
		William Baker
		William Dutton

* Another member of the Chollerton family, John, was a local constable, since records show that in 1857 he was assaulted in the course of his duty by James Barber of Draycott, for which act Barber was given one month's hard labour. It seems sentences had eased off since 1827, when James Price got *two* months' hard labour for stealing two cushions from Charles Holmes of Draycott. (Both these snippets come from Smith [date unknown]).

So there were 36 businesses in Draycott and Church Wilne in 1862, for a combined population of about 1,156 (the 1861 census number). This will be compared with two later 'snapshots', from quite different sources.

Interestingly, *Slater's* also lists the 'gentry' in each township and Draycott notches up two such: Mr William H Scott and Mr John Stevens, though what they had done to warrant their 'Mr' titles is unknown. (Incidentally, the 'gentry' elsewhere did include some women, for example Mrs Elizabeth Stevens of Breaston.) They were probably small landowners, although at this time the Earl of Harrington was still the major local landowner, adding even further to his stock in 1865 with the purchase of most of the former prebendary manor of Sawley from the heirs of the now deceased Rev. Spencer Madan.

One item not noted in *Slater's*, but one which was most definitely visible around this time, was the village gibbet. This is believed to have stood a little beyond the northern boundary of the parish on the lane to Hopwell Hall from the old Derby-Nottingham main road. At least two men are believed to have been hanged there and it is said that some horses still shy when passing the spot where the gibbet stood[1].

Diversity in the church

Not reflected in *Slater's* were the changes afoot in the spiritual rather than the secular world. Founded by John Wesley in 1739, the Methodist movement had become separate from the Church of England by the end of the 18th century and, as we have seen, Draycott's first Methodist church (and the parish's first permanent place of worship outside Wilne) had been built in 1795 as the Wesleyan Chapel on Lodge Street, now Chapel House. This rapidly proved too small and in 1830 a **new Wesleyan Chapel** was built on Victoria Road (now St Mary's C of E Church), large enough to seat 500 and costing £700. A Sunday school was to be added in 1905.

However, the Methodist movement itself had split in 1811 with the emergence of the 'Primitive' Methodists, having a predilection for evangelical outdoor camp meetings, and choosing for themselves a name that today seems oddly self-deprecatory. The Primitives had a

---

[1] Thanks to Max Alexander for information on the village gibbet.

particularly strong following among working-class village communities in the North and Midlands, and Draycott evidently fell into this category, since a **Primitive Chapel** was built in 1854 on Market Street. This original building was converted into a Sunday school in 1897 when a new Primitive Chapel was built on the same site, this latter one still being in use as the Methodist Church today, the various branches of Methodism having reunited in 1932. Among the early preachers at the original Primitive Chapel was Dr Samuel Antliff, who had travelled the world preaching, and in 1884 retired to The Cedars (on the opposite side of Market Street to the chapel); he died in 1891, is buried in Wilne churchyard and, as we see from the inscription on the 'new' chapel, this was built in his memory.

Meanwhile, back in the established Anglican church, the curacy of St Chad's was upgraded to a vicarage in 1865, the vicarage building being what is now Ferristone House on Station Rd. St Chad's was still in the Lichfield diocese until 1884, when it was transferred to the new diocese of Southwell, where it stayed until 1927 when the diocese of Derby was created*. It was therefore the Bishop of Derby who in 1928 dedicated the small **St Mary's Church** on Garfield Avenue (now the senior citizen's hut), before St Mary's moved to the former Wesleyan Chapel building on Victoria Road.

A 'proper' school at last

Now, this to-ing and fro-ing of the various Christian denominations between various buildings in the village had a further significant twist. When the Wesleyan Chapel moved from Lodge Street to Victoria Road in 1830 (see above), the original Lodge Street chapel was converted into a schoolroom, both for the first Methodist Sunday school, with an impressive roll of 140 children, and for **Draycott's first regular day school**, financed by public subscription and with Jonathan James as its first schoolmaster.

This lasted until 1854, when the village's first purpose-built school, the '**National School**', was opened on The Green. (In those days, The

---

* This means that the parish of Draycott and Church Wilne has found itself under five different diocese in its long history: Chester, Lichfield (twice), Coventry, Southwell and Derby.

Green was on the east of The Square, i.e. on the opposite side to where a development of the same name now stands.) The new school cost £900, raised mostly by public subscription but topped up by a government grant, partial state support for education in England having made a hesitant start in 1833. The school's first register showed 120 children in attendance, half of whom were sponsored by Mr Towle of Draycott Mills (not all his own, one assumes!). The National School's first headmaster was Frederick Johnson, with Jane Astle being in charge of infants, but by the time of *Slater's Directory* (1862), these had changed to William Morley and Anne Thompson respectively. Remembering that Draycott's first purpose-built church had been used as a makeshift school, the village's first purpose-built school was now used as a makeshift church! …in winter, for the congregation of St Chad's, where there was no lighting.

The 1870 Education Act made possible the creation of local School Boards and Draycott's board took control of 'the school on the green' in 1876, from when it became known as the Board School. Four years later school attendance became compulsory for five- to twelve-year-olds and in 1891 school fees, which were set at no more than 9d per week, were waived for those without the financial wherewithal.

By the turn of the century, the Board School's premises were becoming a little congested and access to playing fields was difficult, and so a new school building was under construction on its present site of Hopwell Road. The infants' department opened in 1901, but it was to be another four years before the whole school moved across the road. By this time, the 1902 Education Act had swept away the old School Boards and replaced them with Local Education Authorities. In Draycott's case, the LEA was Derbyshire County Council and therefore the new school, officially opened in 1905, was called **Draycott Council School** (as still inscribed in stone on the building's façade), with its first headmaster being Arthur Fell.

Although we're already rather getting ahead of ourselves, it's interesting to read the opinions on the Council School expressed by its own senior pupils in 1953, when they put together a fascinating survey of Draycott, to which we'll return later. They noted that all the classrooms were "large and roomy, with plenty of windows for light and air"[14] (Hazel Smith) and centrally heated, with a fireplace in case the central heating broke down; that in 1935 the lavatories had been converted to WCs; that the wall dividing the boys' from the girls' playground was demolished in 1933; and that "the school has a creditable record in both work and sport" [15] (Ernest Rice). Any current (2001) pupil reading these words may ask themselves what a 'lavatory' was if it wasn't a WC!

According to the 1953 pupils, Draycott school's "most famous scholar" was **William Ewart Bullock** of Breaston who, though his father was "just an ordinary" railwayman, studied at London and Edinburgh Universities and went on to a career in medicine, serving in the Royal Army Medical Corps in the First World War, later specialising in cancer research. Bullock married a suffragette, unusually changed *his* name to *hers* (Gye) and was made a Fellow of the Royal Society in 1938. His father must have had grand plans for his son, naming him after Victorian prime minister William Ewart Gladstone.

The village expands

What other signs of a growing community were to be discerned as the end of the 19th century approached?

Urban residential developments followed the factories, but, in contrast to nearby towns such as Long Eaton, Beeston, Stapleford and Ilkeston, they were on such a small scale in Draycott that the village escaped the urban transformation that overtook its neighbours. Villa Street and part of Harrington Street were built between 1888 and 1890, and then between 1895 and 1900 Fowler Street, and the rest of Harrington Street. Shortly afterwards Town End Road and Sydney Road were built, together with the housing on the north side of Sawley Road. (There was no housing at the time on Elvaston Street.)

In 1902, on the south side of Station Road opposite Harrington Street, Draycott's first motor garage opened for business – Captain M J Astle's **Draycott Motor Company** – and a few doors further west, opposite Town End Road, Mr Antliff[*] the architect opened a new office around the same time. This latter is the small building with the archway that ends the row.

Prompted by the needs of the growing community, the **Draycott Gas Company** was set up in 1887, with its installation north of the railway bridge at end of Town End Road. The company supplied both

---

[*] Grandson of the Methodist preacher.

Draycott and Breaston, including Draycott's first street lighting in 1896.

At the end of 1894, **Draycott Parish Council**[16] was formed, its first meeting, chaired by Marcus Astle, taking place on 3rd January 1895 in the Board School on The Green. However, the creation of the council had not taken place without controversy. On 4th December 1894, a parish meeting had been called at the same location to elect the councillors, and the chairman of that meeting, Mr J Allport, first announced that of the 16 nominations, that of Alfred Smith was invalid, being proposed by a "non-elector". The remaining 15 candidates were put before the meeting, the votes for them carefully counted and the top seven announced, in order of popularity, as:

- Samuel Moore
- Marcus Astle
- Robert Johnson
- Arthur Hill
- Joseph Cooper
- Thomas Youngman
- George Gilbert

(The days of women councillors were evidently a long way off.)

At 8:42 pm Mr Allport gave the assembly ten minutes in which to demand a poll of the village, otherwise the above seven would form the council. At 8:43 pm Mr Jesse Statham demanded a poll. Despite being "addressed by Messrs Johnson, Wootton, Gilbert and Dudgeon to induce him to withdraw his demand", Mr Statham did not do so and so a poll was held. The subsequent poll removed Messrs Youngman and Gilbert from the list, replacing them with Messrs Wootton and Maltby. Quite what controversies underlay these events we can only guess. One clue is that the public poll showed Marcus Astle to be by far and away the most popular candidate, after his having come only second in the parish meeting (to Samuel Moore). As Captain Astle is believed to have been both influential and popular in Church Wilne, perhaps the location of the parish meeting in Draycott had under-represented the electors from this distant outpost of the parish.

In 1906, the council moved its meeting room to the new Council School on Hopwell Road and then in 1974 to its current home in the Parish Rooms (the former telephone exchange) on Elvaston Street.

The minutes of early Parish Council meetings reveal the solution to the mystery of Market Street, raised earlier. There did indeed used to be a **market** held in the wide area that some locals still refer to as the Market Place, but which is now usually known as The Square. The evidence is to be found in the reports of the council's Shows and Markets Committee, whose scale of charges to stallholders make it quite clear that, at least in 1896, these events were rather more 'show' than 'market':

"Cocoa nut alleys, football kicking or lotteries: 2/-
Swing boats, small, per boat: 1/-
Shooting galleries, per tube: 3/6
Roundabouts, up to 15 feet in diameter: 3/-"[17]

However there must have been some regular market stalls, as in 1897 the council resolved to increase the charges for "butchers, drapers, provision dealers etc."[18] to 2/6, which incidentally was also the payment made to the person with the unenviable task of cleaning up the Market Place after Saturday markets, which we must therefore assume were the messiest. The existence of regular food stalls at the market is confirmed by one villager who specifically remembers buying a pomegranate there in 1917!

1899 saw the construction of a row of shops in front of 'The City', which was an older group of shops and cottages on what is now The Green. The 1899 row was built on the site of an old woodyard and is still there (containing Barney's store).

Along Derby Road some 'ribbon' development had already begun along the north side, with two short terraces having been built either side of the old factory, by then the Unionist Club, followed by three detached residences standing back from the road at this time. All these still stand and in 1899 would have had views across the fields to the river, since the south side was almost entirely open: between New Street and the railway bridge there stood only Rose Cottage, now Number 47 Derby Road, and one more house, now demolished, just before the bridge. This was to change with the construction from 1900 of Garfield Avenue, Cleveland Avenue and Lime Grove, the first two being named after U.S. presidents of the preceding twenty years.

Along Hopwell Road, we've already seen that the Council School was opened in 1901 and extended in 1905. Further along, the cemetery and its chapel were also built in 1901, relieving congestion in Wilne churchyard, and in 1904 – for those in a slightly better condition – the

Isolation Hospital was built further along the road, beyond Draycott Fields Farm. This formed part of Shardlow Joint Hospital District and could accommodate up to 32 patients suffering from diptheria or scarlet fever. By 1953 it had expanded its capacity to 50 patients (now including tuberculosis sufferers too) and 30 staff. A patient from the 1960s[*] recalls the hospital's cold atmosphere, which they were told was as a vital part of the treatment! At the time of writing, the old hospital is being converted to a collection of 'executive dwellings'.

---

[*] Reported by Janet Shaw.

Victoria Mills, early 1900s, with Sydney Street under construction.
Photo: Long Eaton Library.

Draycott Council School, infants' class, 1928.
Photo: Long Eaton Library

5. All Hands to the Pump (1908 – 1953)

As if the Great War wasn't enough…

Having found its way onto the industrial map with the official opening of Victoria Mills in 1908, Draycott thrived for a while on the lace trade. By 1916 there were 17 lace firms operating in the village. Diversion of commercial enterprises towards the war effort was evidently less marked in the 1914-18 conflict than in 1939-45. In fact, whereas we can learn something of the effects of the Second World War on village life from personal accounts (see later), little has been recorded of local events during the Great War, apart from the 56 local men killed in action and commemorated at the war memorial on Station Road. Two exceptions however are two more disastrous fires, unrelated to the war but of great significance to the local community. Both were in Church Wilne, but appear to have been unconnected.

The first was in March 1917 at St Chad's church. The only two causes mooted were a deliberate act of sabotage by the Suffragettes and a stray cigarette end. Since at the time virtually every calamity drew accusations against the Suffragette movement – and since there is no record of any evidence in this direction – the second can be taken as the most likely. Despite the best efforts of the Derby fire brigade, and though no-one was hurt, the resulting fire was catastrophic to the church's interior, where the old oak roof and two oak screens were destroyed, many church treasures were destroyed or damaged, including the old Anglo-Saxon font, which was broken into several pieces. The tower and most of the other external structure, however, survived relatively unscathed. With resources for repair work not easily available because of the war effort, the interior remained in its blackened state for some time. Eventually, after six years and £7,000, the restored building – complete with new oak roof – re-opened for services in 1923. Oddly enough, not everyone was happy about this. A number of parishioners had baulked at investing in the church at Wilne when there was still no Anglican church in Draycott, but as we have already seen they had to endure only five more years of The Great Trek until the first St Mary's opened for business on Garfield Avenue.

Back in 1917, on a balmy evening in June, fire struck yet again. This time the scene was at Wilne Mills, owned at the time by Marcus Astle, and still engaged principally in cotton manufacturing. Only 12 people were in the factory that evening and none was injured, but this time the Derby fire engine was not given permission to attend and so it was left to the fireman of Shardlow to tackle the blaze. Unfortunately all they had at their disposal were a hand engine and a few extinguishers. They evidently found themselves up against it: the five-storey main building was gutted; 15,000 spindles and a great deal of cotton were destroyed; and 140 workers found themselves out of a job. Reconstruction didn't even start until 1923, when the new structure, now much larger but comprising only two storeys, was built on piers of reinforced concrete pipes from Stanton, with concrete foundations actually lower than the river bed. It re-opened the next year and the main 1924 building still forms part of the Wilne Mills complex today, where the piers are still clearly visible from the public road.

Astle took the opportunity to update almost the entire plant and machinery at the mill, buying new clearing, gassing and reeling machines and new doubling frames, all from Stubbs of Manchester. A short paper written by Astle himself in 1924[19] veritably bristles with his pride in all the new equipment, not least the electric plant supplied by Harvey of Nottingham, which remarkably included one dynamo still driven by the mill's water wheel. Power efficiency was vital as the price of coal had increased threefold from its pre-war price.

The lessons to be learned from the delays in dealing with three catastrophic local fires over a period of 15 years eventually sank in: in 1928, after much debate, the Parish Council finally decided to cease their payments to Long Eaton Fire Brigade and bought some fire-fighting equipment of their own. This was stationed at Victoria Mills (no doubt still regarded as the greatest local risk) and placed under the supervision of their engineer Mr Haywood. He and his men soon received a hand cart with which to manoeuvre the fire appliances and found themselves dealing with all the village's fire emergencies, the first recorded of which was a haystack fire on South Street.

The Draycott Gas War and other developments

In Draycott, unlike Church Wilne, new sources of employment

continued to pop up during the inter-war years, despite the economic problems that seemed to have beset the nation as a whole. The 1920s saw The Draycott Hosiery Company set up business in Draycott Mills (1926) and John Skerritt built his single-storey textile factory (**Skerritt's Mill**) on Walter Street (1929). During the following decade Skerritt expanded with another building on the same site (1935) and Turner's lace company set up shop in Draycott Mills (1936), although, as we've seen with respect to Victoria Mills, the lace trade as a whole had entered a decline soon after the first war.

Skerritt's Mill was at the centre of the main housing developments in the village between the wars. Some houses next to the factory on Walter Street were built around the same time as the factory itself (1929) and Gertrude Road, Arthur Street, West Avenue and the rest of Walter Street followed during the 1930s. Gertrude, Arthur and Walter were members of Skerritt's family.

On the north side of Derby Road itself, the individual houses that fill in the second half of the stretch to the railway bridge were built before the first war. On the south side, the housing on Garfield Avenue, Cleveland Avenue and Lime Grove, having been only partly built before the war, was completed after it.

In the meantime a rather more localised war had broken out: the Draycott Gas War. There had been a gradual growth in demand for town gas, at first just for street lighting, and then for domestic lighting, cooking and heating. Around the turn of the century the Long Eaton Gas Company had installed mains in Draycott, in direct competition with the supply from the Draycott Gas Company which, as we have seen, had been in operation from its works beyond the railway since 1887. By 1908, the local company was endeavouring, through legal means, to compel the intruder to remove its mains from Draycott's streets, but significantly Long Eaton gas was the cheaper. Partially in an attempt to bring down unit costs, the Draycott company expanded its operations by taking over the Castle Donington Gas Company and supplying the whole of its new empire from the Draycott works. Hoist by its own petard, however, the Draycott company was itself taken over by the Long Eaton company in 1922. The Draycott gasometer remained in place beyond Villa Street at least until the 1930s and Draycott's gas showrooms, in the tall building on Victoria Road that now contains The Hair Studio, for considerably longer.

Draycott was first connected to mains electricity in the 1930s, but even well after the second war Derek Orchard, of Orchard's electrical shop on Market Street, can recall the regular visits to many local properties that were not connected, in order to charge their 'wet' batteries with his 'accumulator'.

Draycott's first telephone exchange was installed in Sydney Road around this time – in Mr Hughes' front room! Before the Second World War he had to deal with only a dozen or so phone lines in the entire village. Eventually a puropose-built exchange on Elvaston Street (now the Parish Rooms) finally relieved the congestion in Mr Hughes' house.

The 1930s also saw serious flooding in the area; for example, the the basement of the old chapel (now church) on Victoria Road is believed to have been regularly inundated at this time.

Life in the 1930s[20]

As we have mentioned, this part of the country appears not to have been so badly hit by recession in the 1930s as other parts of Britain and indeed many local people look back on the immediate pre-war years with affection. There certainly seems to have been plenty to do, especially for youngsters.

Derbyshire Education Committee purchased land on the opposite side of Hopwell Road to give the school its first playing field. Bounded by the road and the railway, plus Mr Wallis' field to the east and Mr Fritchley's field to the south, the playing field included a tennis court on its east side and a school garden by the railway. We learn from the pupils' post-war survey that it measured exactly 1 acre, 1 rood and 33¼ square poles (the field evidently contributing to maths lessons as well). However, according to the same pupils, it was "not quite big enough" for football or athletics, and "rather too rough"[21] for cricket.

Outside school, there was a string of annual events which the children must have looked forward to with eagerness. Two **wakes** (fairs)*

---

*   Although 'shows and markets' were still permitted on the Market Place as late as 1930, no reports were made by the council's Shows and Markets Committee after that date, and so we may assume that the Market Street venue was no longer used for this purpose.

used to arrive in Draycott in the autumn, a week before the Nottingham Goose Fair. Holland's Wakes was on the field to the north of Victoria Road (now the site of Astec's car park); the other, larger, wakes was Hibbles and Mellors', creating an island of bright lights and music on Billy West's field beyond the end of Town End Road. One enthusiastic visitor to the wakes was young Joyce Haywood (now Barton), who remembers the dodgems, the cake-walk, the skittles, the coconut shies, the steam engines and the horses; another was Grace Gaskin, who remembers the intriguingly named 'chair-o-planes'; and Ron Mason and Barry Fletcher both remember the swingboats – from which it was rumoured that coins occasionally fell out of the patrons' pockets onto the grass below! One of the fairground showmen, a Mr Bishton, actually lived permanently in Draycott, in a caravan behind The Traveller's Rest on Clay Street.

Not long after the wakes came Bonfire Night, with sticky toffee, corned-beef pies, Dad's old clothes on the guy... and unfortunately one year the accidental burning down of a Dutch barn at Slater's Farm! After the fun of Christmas, the New Year, snowballing and Easter came the annual **Draycott Carnival**, organised to raise extra money for hospitals. The carnival parade, and especially the carnival queen and her attendants, drew most of the village to the streets and used to finish on the field that is now the Hopwell Road sports field. Although individual parades (for example, by the local Conservatives or by the Spondon Legionnaires) still continued into the 1980s, the generic village event petered out in the 1970s.

Warm summer days brought plenty of opportunity for fun and games on a rather less organised scale. The village children used to learn to swim in the canal, running over Mr Slater's fields with their 'cossies', towels, bottles of tea and lemonade, maybe taking a diversion to donate a few cakes to the greengrocer's horse... until Mr Cartrwright chased everyone away. The fields around Draycott and Church Wilne were also full of excellent spots for a picnic – and maybe the chance of earning a penny by opening the gate on Wilne Road for a passing car or cart. As autumn approached, the children would also look forward to pitching in with the harvest work – well, more fun than work when you're a youngster. As the nights closed in, there was still plenty of entertainment available at home, from board games (e.g. Ludo or Lotto) to hide and seek. In the 1930s (as indeed through to the 1950s), entertainment for children was still something to be created for themselves, not provided on tap.

So what did the youths and adults get up to, out of working hours, while the children were entertaining themselves? Well, among the activities today's locals recall (and will admit to!) are the dance club; the chance of a flutter on the horses at big Ben Kirk's (illegal) bookie's hut where McNeil Grove is now built; the evening motor-bike outings; and the opportunities for a gossip outside one or other of the village chip shops – one on the corner of New Street, one opposite the Coach & Horses (Bob Statham's) and one on Station Road opposite Fowler Street (Mr Seal's). Of course, on fine days there was plenty of scope for country walks and bike rides in all directions – including south, as the Draycott chain ferry still operated between the Ferry House and the Ambaston bank, and further downstream Wilne Bridge gave access to the Shardlow bank. And for those who were 'in' with the hunting set, the Earl of Harrington's hunt still met in the 1930s outside the church at Wilne.

A mini-snapshot of Church Wilne

One of the dwindling number of Church Wilne's inhabitants at this time, Florence Tideswell (now Clay), has written up her own memories of Wilne between the wars[22] and what follows is a brief summary of these revealing documents.

Church Wilne's population (exact year unknown) was 90, living in 18 homes, and not surprisingly everyone knew everyone else by name. A list, also prepared by Mrs Clay, of the residents over a number of years reveals a number of large families: there were 11 Battelles, 9 Hawkins, 9 Muglestons, 9 Wilmots (including those at the toll house) and 7 Rodbers. Also appearing are Marcus and Priscilla Astle, owners of Wilne Mill and landlords for many of Wilne's houses; the Astles themselves seem to have divided their time between their house at the mill and Attewell House in Draycott.

The nearby church evidently carried a strong influence, expecially on the older residents. Among the many local characters were an old, white-bearded gentleman who rewarded village children with sweets for perfectly recited passages from the Bible, and an old lady who would give a quick pinch to any girls failing to wear white on Whit Sunday!

While day-to-day life became a little easier up the road in Draycott, with the gradual arrival of more convenient services, life in Church Wilne was still something of a struggle. In the continued absence of a piped water supply, several hand pumps were still situated around the hamlet to draw water from nearby wells, and rain butts caught the rainwater running off the roof tops. For longer than in Draycott, wood and coal were the only sources of heat, and candles and oil lamps the only sources of light at night. Even when gas arrived, the light afforded on the lane by gas lamps was shortlived due to damage by vandals. Laundry was washed in a coal-fired copper and ironed with a flat iron heated in the fireplace.

Every Thursday's arrival of the horse-drawn Co-op cart with its grocery orders was vital, as was the twice-weekly service from the hand-drawn Co-op bread cart. Dairy produce was a little easier, with milk from either of the village's two farms – one next to the church and the other near the mill – being supplied door-to-door, directly from pail to jug, and butter, cream and eggs being available for purchase at a house on the mill site. Perhaps the longest supply route was the lane from Shardlow, which once a week saw a pony and trap in charge of a chap known to all as 'Barmo', bringing just one product: yeast. Going in the other direction, though probably not on Barmo's cart, were osiers (willow shoots) from osier beds near the church, destined for use in Shardlow's basket-making trade.

No bus service ever reached Wilne… to this day. The reality of this situation before widespread car ownership is brought home by the recollection of young Florence Tideswell's journeys to and from Draycott school. The trudge up or down the unsurfaced lane took 20 minutes and, astonishing as it may seem to today's youngsters, there were no school dinners to be had[*] and so the walk was made not twice but *four* times a day, in all weathers. No wonder a passing cart was such a welcome sight… whatever may have been the other contents of the cart, and whatever the views of Mr Lager, the headmaster, on the arrival at school of the Wilne contingent!

In fact, the commonly held belief that the gradual abandonment of

---

[*] Draycott School served its first school meals in 1943.

Church Wilne was down to a constant flood threat is questioned by Mrs Clay: the sheer inconvenience of living in a tiny hamlet with so few services and, the mill apart, with no employment opportunities, simply drove the youngsters away and with them the community itself.

Living in Wilne, however, did bring some compensations. St Chad's, then as now, was regularly used for concerts and the sounds of violin, cello, organ, choir and a number of solo voices must have rung clearly around the village. Moreover, as most of the residents at this time were tenants of Captain Astle, not only was their passage over the Wilne Toll Bridge free but also it is believed they were given special permission to use the private path that at one time led from Wilne Road directly to Astle's Attewell House... which, when you were literally running late, could mean the difference between getting to the railway station on time and missing your train!

Draycott at war

The Second World War had a more direct effect on Britain's towns and villages than the First, partly due to air raids, both threatened and real.

Responsible for ensuring local blackouts and air-raid warnings was the Air-Raid Protection (ARP) warden at Rose Cottage (now 47 Derby Road), where Draycott's air-raid siren was also located. In the field at the back (now Thoresby Crescent) was the searchlight station. This time Draycott had its own temporary fire station, located in the yard of Draycott Mills and proud operators of a Coventry Climax pump and Vauxhall motor car. The Home Guard was led by Sergeant Farmer and met in Wilne Church; and Draycott House, on Hopwell Road, was converted into a temporary military hospital.

The rumour in the village was that German bombers used the green dome of Victoria Mills as a landmark, before banking west or east for raids on Derby or Nottingham/Chilwell, but in fact there were apparently only two cases of strikes in the Draycott and Church Wilne area, possibly in error, the bombs falling mostly in fields. They did *not* however prove harmless, as two local children were later killed by unexploded bombs on the ground. There were indeed a number of potential targets here: the businesses on the Draycott Mills site produced munitions, 20-mm shells and aero parts, as well as the shell-testing site at Bliss's in what is now

Cee Bee Garage. However, the area was obviously regarded as relatively safe, since a number of evacuees from Sheffield were billeted in Draycott, some of them working in the temporary munitions factories here.

Rationing of course had a direct effect on all local families, including the children, whose supply of chocolates and sweets now depended on coupons. The fuel shortage prompted the closure of Bird's Garage (previously Astle's 1902 garage) and its conversion into a shop by Mr Page. And again, inevitably, the village lost some of its young men in action: this time 12 were killed.

Although rationing continued until the early 1950s for some produce, Draycott and Church Wilne rapidly picked themselves up after the conflict, dusted themselves down and got back to 'business as usual'. Most of the industrial resources diverted to the war effort returned to their peacetime operations. The former Draycott Motor Company garage on Station Road changed use yet again, this time in 1947 to a small textile factory – Astrand Mills – once again under the ownership of the Astle family. In 1949 Wilne Mills was taken over for the production of fireworks, a trade that is continued there to this day by 'pyrotechnic manufacturers' Haley & Weller Ltd. And all over Britain, sports enthusiasts emerged from the restrictions of wartime in great shape (see later).

A post-war snapshot

As already mentioned, in 1953 the 'Senior Scholars' of Draycott Council School undertook a detailed survey of Draycott and Church Wilne, as part of an historical study not unlike this one, documenting their findings in a small booklet which gives us a post-war snapshot to compare with the rather less reliable one of 1862 (see above) and with a current one (see later).

The table below has been compiled from the 1953 study, with detail added by Derek Orchard. Those shops marked with an asterisk were also in existence before the war, according to a list compiled by Lou Haywood.

Businesses in Draycott and Church Wilne, 1953			
Category	Business	Name	Location

Industry	Textiles	[Unnamed]	Victoria Mills
		[Unnamed]	Victoria Mills
		[Unnamed]	Victoria Mills
		[Unnamed]	Victoria Mills
		[Unnamed]	Victoria Mills
		[Unnamed]	Victoria Mills
		[Unnamed]	Victoria Mills
		[Unnamed]	Victoria Mills
		[Unnamed]	Victoria Mills
		[Unnamed]	Astrand Mills
		Fletcher's	Draycott Mills
		Skerritt's	Skerritt's Mills
	Explosives	Haley and Weller	Wilne Mills
	Engineering	Parry's	Victoria Mills
Shops	Grocer	Griffiths*	Wilne Rd
		Co-op*	Market St
		Alton & Priesthall	Market St
		Matthews	Derby Rd
		Stevenson*	Victoria Rd
		Lewis	Victoria Rd
		Dexter	Victoria Rd
		Berrisford*	Station Rd
		Gilbert	Sydney Rd
	Butcher	Co-op *	Market St
		Fritchley*	Victoria Rd
		Bunting (or Slater*?)	Victoria Rd
		Morgan	Station Rd
	Greengrocer	Co-op*	Market Street
		Smith*	Station Rd
	Wines and Spirits	Warhurst*	Station Rd
	Confectioner	Savage*	Market St
		[Unnamed] (Winfield*?) (Coutts*?) (Harris*?)	

		(Gilbert*?)	
	Cobbler	Bisnal	Market St
		[Unnamed] (Lambert*?)	
	Draper	White*	Victoria Rd
		[Unnamed] (Chapman*?)	
	Woollens	Orchard*	Station Rd
	Newsagent	Teece(*?)	Victoria Rd
		Harris	Station Rd
	'General'	Atkin*	Station Rd
		Lodge*	Victoria Rd
	Postal services	Post Office (Shaw)*	Victoria Rd
	Stationer	Tizzard	Station Rd
	Chemist	Marsh	Station Rd
	Gas appliances	Long Eaton Gas Company*	Victoria Rd
	Cycles and electrical goods	Orchard*	Market St
		Chamberlain	South St
	Handicraft	Hollas	Victoria Rd
	Decorating materials	Wigley	Station Rd
	Building materials	Harrison	Station Rd
Catering	Pub	Traveller's Rest	Derby Rd
		Victoria Hotel	Victoria Rd
		Coach & Horses	Victoria Rd
		Draycott Hotel	Station Rd
		Rose & Crown	Market St
	Cafe	Casey	Market St
	Takeaway	Seal*	Derby Rd
Other services	Bank	Barclays*	Station Rd
	Hairdresser	Sanderson	Station Rd
		[Unnamed]	

| | | (Cobb*?) | |

Shops that had apparently disappeared* since before the war included Anderton's fish and chip shop on Sydney Road, Bob Statham's fish and chip shop on Victoria Road, Cooper's potted meat shop on Station Road and 'Flip It' Cartwright's greengrocery on The Green (with his mobile pony and trap).

The factories the school survey recorded were:
- Victoria Mills, employing 293 people.
- Draycott Mills, employing 126 people.
- Wilne Mills, employing 100 people.
- Astrand Mills, employing 31 people.
- Skerritt's Mills, employing 25 people.

In fact, Victoria Mills comprised ten businesses: five lace firms, four other textile firms and Parry's electrical engineers. Draycott Mills, then as now, was also a multi-business site, but their number was not recorded; for the sake of a little calculation, let's assume there were four businesses there. We also have to add the five pubs in 1953 – The Draycott Hotel (Olympic), The Old Coach and Horses, The Victoria Hotel, The Traveller's Rest and The Rose & Crown. Finally, we must add the gasworks. This gives us a grand (estimated) total of 63 businesses in Draycott and Church Wilne for a population of 2,140; compared with the 1862 figures of 36 for 1,156. The population had grown by 185% and the number of businesses by 175%; so, on this crude measure, Draycott at least was still pretty well-provided with services.

Looking back at the *types* of business in 1862, only 16 were what might be described as shops, and so it's interesting to note that the number of shops had made a disproportionate jump of 225%, to 36. In fact, at this time, Draycott had more shops than neighbouring Breaston, even though the latter had a greater population.

Perhaps the most notable feature of the *location* of businesses is that by 1953 the Victoria Road–Station Road axis was almost completely dominant, the only exception being the cluster of shops around The Square: Mr Orchard had bought the whole row of shops on the west side just after the war, running the electrical shop in that row with his son, and opposite these stood the Co-op, since demolished and its site now

---

* Comparing Lou Haywood's pre-war list with the school's post-war list.

occupied by new housing and a small area of greenery. South Street, once the village's bustling main street, could boast only a single surviving shop in the 1953 survey – Chamberlain's radio and TV store on the corner with Market Street – although Griffiths' grocery shop ('The Barn') also survived further out along Wilne Road.

By now, the local factories drew in employees from the surrounding area, including from Shardlow via the toll bridge at Wilne. Mr Gidlow, the Co-op manager, is also believed to have come to work this way on his bicycle. Church Wilne itself, however, had shrunk even further, the 1953 survey recording just 12 houses and 28 inhabitants in the hamlet.

Other miscellaneous remarks by the 1953 pupils remind us how, while some things have changed beyond recognition in the last fifty years, others sound very familiar:

- Draycott had regular bus services in both Derby and Nottingham directions every 15 minutes.
- Draycott & Breaston railway station was still in operation, by now under the nationalised British Railways, with seven trains a day to Derby, and eleven in the opposite direction.
- There was a mixture of gas and electric lighting in Draycott's houses. Some were still on the old penny gas meter, although the majority by then used the shilling meter. Most domestic electricity was also paid for by shilling meters, although some advanced – or reckless! – householders had graduated to quarterly bills.
- One pupil (David Mends) had a lot to say about street lighting, where he noted that Draycott was badly in need of "a big improvement". The only electric street lighting in 1953 was to be found along the main roads, plus one light on Walter Street, and the only location where they stayed on all night was at the junction of Station Road and Sawley Road. It's possible that, with the long memory of the wartime blackout, night-time lighting was still something of a novelty, and the concept of urban lighting as a form of 'pollution' evidently still a long way off.
- By 1953, Draycott and Church Wilne's telephone count had risen to 96, a number still small enough to be listed in

their entirety in just half a page of the pupils' survey. Only 40 of the numbers were at domestic addresses, i.e. at only 6% of the 662 houses, and so the ownership of a telephone was still very much something of a status symbol. However, a direct link to today's situation is to be found in the numbers themselves, some of which have simply gained a few preceding digits; for example, in 1953 The Traveller's Rest was Draycott 332 and today it is Derby 872332.

So, although some of the technology in early 1950s Draycott may seem a little quaint from the perspective of the 21st century, it's clear that many of the key elements that were subsequently to change the nature of everyday life for many villagers were already in place soon after the war. This includes the single most influential piece of technology, which was however oddly absent from the 1953 study and whose influence opens our final chapter.

*'Downtown' Church Wilne, date unknown.
(Photo: Long Eaton Library)*

6. Commuter Territory (1954 – 2000)

The creeping conquest of the car

Car ownership in Britain began to take off in the 1950s, accelerated in the 1960s and then continued its remorseless rise to the end of the century. Some towns were virtually created by the car, others transformed and even in nearby Long Eaton, the jams, the parking and the ubiquitous speed bumps now regularly top the list of issues guaranteed to get the greatest number of locals hottest under the collar. If a Draycott child of the 1930s had fallen asleep for sixty years and woken up in the 1990s, there's no doubt that the single most shocking change to the village would have been the traffic. However – and I realise I may be swimming against the tide here – I suggest that in many ways Draycott has 'got off rather lightly' in this respect.

It can't be denied that turn-of-the-century Draycott is partly a dormitory suburb of Derby, Nottingham, and to a lesser extent Long Eaton, and it does indeed have its morning and evening rush hours; but the fact that the local commuters drive off in virtually every direction, combined with the village's simultaneous role as a *recipient* of daily commuters, means that the rush hours do not generate any *single* major traffic flow. Indeed, an actual traffic jam is a rare site in Draycott and the fact that the village still has only one set of traffic lights – and that for the convenience of school-bound pedestrians – bears witness to the relative lack of *real* traffic problems. The same is true of the parking situation: although a significant proportion of the village's housing stock is still pre-car and therefore garageless, these dwellings are spread around the village and there's always a parking space within a few yards of anyone's destination, whether home or shop.

However, three side-effects of the post-war car culture *have* had significant effects on both Draycott and Church Wilne, and they're not particularly beneficial:

- First, Draycott & Breaston railway station finally closed in 1966, due to increasing competition from both car and bus. In 2001, local inhabitants have to travel to Long Eaton or Derby for the nearest railway service, but the good news is that 1999 saw a dramatic increase in direct Midland

Mainline services to London from both these stations.
- Second, the explosion of supermarkets in the surrounding area, but not in Draycott itself, has led to the conecpt of the weekly shop and the consequent decline and disappearance of many of the village's own food shops. As the survey below reveals, between 1953 and 2000, while the population steadily increased, the combined total of grocers, greengrocers and butchers in the village shrank from 15 to 4.
- And third, the particular version of car crime that has recently hit this area combines the theft, abandonment and burning of vehicles down otherwise quiet country lanes, the targets around here being the two lanes leading to Church Wilne. At the time of writing there are three burnt-out wrecks within a few hundred yards of Wilne church, one having been there for almost a year and the most recent arrival being a (barely recognisable) ambulance.

That sporting life

As already noted, sport flourished after the war and, possibly thanks to the initial efforts of two outstanding sports masters at the Council School – Mr Hackett and Mr Horner – some sporting heroes began to emerge. Local lad Fred Smith, a Draycott Youth Club leader, played football for Sheffield United; Terry Springthorpe appeared in the 1949 FA Cup Final for Wolverhampton Wanderers; John Winfield was a regular full-back for Nottingham Forest during the 1960s; Alan Revill played cricket for Derbyshire; and Betty Archer (now Betty Fletcher) ran for Derbyshire at Eton in the 1940s. Brief details of selected local sports stars appear below[*].

As far as team performances are concerned, the outstanding tale must be that of **Draycott Amateurs FC**, who dominated local amateur football for ten years from 1953. Having won the Long Eaton League in 1953-4, they entered Section C of the Derby Senior League for the 1954-5 season, finishing runners-up in both League and Cup and winners of the Medal competition. Promoted to Section B, Draycott took the division

---

[*] Many thanks to Ron Mason for assembling these details.

apart, dropping only one point all season and notching up a 15-0 away victory over Brighton Road Old Boys, a record-breaking 8 (eight!) goals coming from winger Barry Fletcher, a record that still stands. So 1956-57 saw them in Section A. After an inauspicious start of two defeats in two games, Draycott 'Ams' quickly got the measure of the new standard and took the top local amateur league by storm, conceding no more defeats all season and winning not just the Championship but also the League Cup and the Divisional Cup (South): a sensational performance from a special side.

For this achievement, each player received a Crown Derby plate and £1 from Mr Dexter, the manager of Haley & Weller (the firework factory), who had also boosted the team's efforts with a prize of 10 shillings per goal... Draycott *Amateurs*?! Among the team members that still live in the village are Barry Fletcher and full-back Ron Mason, who remember fondly the exceptional team spirit and enthusiastic local support that contributed to their success. In fact, the double-decker bus that carried the Draycott supporters to one away match at Gresley Rovers was so full that the driver asked the standing passengers to lay on the floor as they passed through towns, lest the police stop them for overfilling the vehicle!

Draycott Amateurs used to play on Gamble's field (now occupied by Thoresby Crescent), where nearby sheds occasionally bore the brunt of some wayward shots on goal. Draycott Swifts and Draycott Rovers used to play football on the 'Leg of Mutton' field, just before 'Whitegates' on the north side of Sawley Road, and Draycott Women's Hockey Club used to use a nearby field off the south side of Station Road.

Draycott Cricket Club, then as now, played on what one of the 1953 pupils called "by far the best sports ground in the parish"[23]: the pitch behind the school off Hopwell Road. This club was formed in 1898, when George Travers won the Marcus Astle Trophy for batting, and three years later the first winner of the club's A T Alton Trophy for bowling was Ernest Gutteridge. In the postwar years, Draycott CC's fixtures were strictly friendlies, though none the less keenly played for that, their 1956 opponents including, for example, Breaston, Kedleston, Long Eaton Old Boys and – the team that always brought the biggest and most vocal support – West Indian Caribs. Being regularly rolled and treated with marl, the Hopwell Road pitch had a reputation as an excellent batting track, exemplified by one six that ended up not only across the road but also across the railway and in the cemetery! Surviving members from the 1950s team remember when a certain relaxed fielder, known to pass the time while fielding in the deep by enjoying the occasional cigarette, was literally sparked into action one day when, turning to chase a ball to the boundary, he found that the matches in his pocket had ignited and set his cricket trousers alight!

The Draycott sports club that many outsiders will know is **Draycott Boxing Club**. Founded in 1967 after a meeting at the Rose & Crown, it was officially opened the next year by Jack Bodell, who was to become British Heavyweight Champion the following year. At this time, the boxing took place at The Welfare Centre (the former church on Garfield Avenue, now the Senior Citizens Club), but in 1975 the club moved across to the new premises that later housed the youth club, this building being officially opened by Derby County and Nottingham Forest striker John O'Hare.

Careers of some of Draycott's sports stars

John Kennedy, boxer
Member of Draycott Boxing Club.
Trained by local ABA coach Tony Wall[*].
As amateur, won all 12 international contests.
1979: turned professional with Sam Burns of London.

Garnet Lee, cricketer
Landlord of the Traveller's Rest.
1925-33: Derbyshire Cricket Club.
Scored over 1000 runs in six consecutive seasons.
1927: took 72 wickets.

---

[*] Thanks to Draycott's own boxing judge, referee and coach, Tony Wall, for compiling the boxing information.

Alan Revill, cricketer
President of Draycott Cricket Club.
1946-57: Derbyshire Cricket Club.
Scored over 1000 runs in seven consecutive seasons.
Took 396 catches in career. (1952: 45 in one season)

Fred Smith, footballer
1947: Derby County.
1948: Sheffield Utd.
1952: Manchester City.
1952: Grimsby Town.
1954: Bradford City.
1954: Frickley Colliery.

Terry Springthorpe, footballer
1936-7: Draycott Schoolboys (coach: H. Horner)
1937-9: Draycott Juniors (coach: J. Stubbs)
1939: Signed by Wolverhampton Wanderers at age 16.
1939-41: Wolves' left-back in Wartime League.
(1942-6: Wartime service: RASC, North Africa, Italy, Palestine)
1946-50: Resumed career with Wolves, sharing lodgings with Billy Wright.
1949: Appeared for Wolves in their 3-1 FA Cup Final win over Leicester City.
1950-51: Coventry City.
1951: Emigrated to USA.
1951-2: Fall River Indians.
1952-62: New York Americans.
1953: Played for USA in their 3-6 defeat by England (captained by Billy Wright).
1954/58: Played for USA in World Cup qualifiers.
1962: Returned to England.
1962-4: Notts Amateurs (Midland League).

A. Winfield, boxer
Member of Draycott Boxing Club.
Trained by A. Juffs.
1971: reached ABA semi-finals.
1972: turned professional with Clive Hall of Kettering.

John Winfield, footballer
1961-73: full back for Nottingham Forest.
Scored on his debut at age 17.
Career: 408 games, 5 goals.

Filling in and mopping up

In the world of housing, the last four decades of the 20th century saw the piecemeal replacement of some older housing and the gradual encroachment of Draycott's housing onto a few more erstwhile fields and gardens, though once again on a very small scale compared with the fate suffered by some neighbouring communities. In the mid-sixties, Coulson's Yard and some Market Street properties were demolished and Milner Avenue built in their place, followed by the demolition of Holly House, next to the Rose & Crown, and the construction of Holly Close and McNeil Grove on its extensive former grounds. The developments at the southern ends of Lime Grove, Cleveland Avenue and Garfield Avenue also appeared stage-by-stage around this time, including the controversy over a proposed end-on access between St Mary Avenue / Queen's Court and Milner Avenue, a matter which rumbled on until settled definitively by the erection of the sturdy concrete wall that still separates these two developments. Older properties were also replaced during the 1960s, '70s and '80s along Victoria Road, South Street, Walk Close and Derwent Street, where much of Draycott Hall's gardens were sold for new housing.

Down the lane in Church Wilne, it was more a question of digging out than filling in, for it was Hoveringham's gravel extraction project that sounded the death knell for most of the hamlet's remaining buildings. The group of old cottages situated just to the south of the bridleway to Breaston and known as New Delight (reason unknown, even to one of its erstwhile residents) had disappeared some time since. And then it is believed that the 1964 acquisitions by Hoveringham led to the demolition of the three remaining cottages and various farm buildings abutting the north side of the churchyard. In fact the air vents from the former cattle stalls can still be seen in the church-side of the wall between churchyard and car park.

This left just the mill, the church and the two detached houses we see today. These latter were built by the Astles in 1925 as four semis for millworkers. Though still marked on maps as Armiston Cottages, they were not known as such when built and are not physically marked as such now. It's interesting to note that the desirability of 'remote' homes seems to be increasing, as measured by the recent asking price of over £200,000 for one of these cottages. In fact recent years have seen a number of enquiries for planning permission to build in or around Church Wilne, but the hamlet's chances of a renaissance are slim, since the Environment Agency has recommended against development in this part of the Derwent flood plain.

On the roads, the 1960s saw the rebuilding and realignment of the Derby Road railway bridge (where the old right-angled alignment is still visible to the south) and the complete demolition of Hopwell Road canal bridge, as the Derby Canal had by then fallen into disuse.

Actually, one relatively recent development has finally put Draycott at the top of a nation-wide – indeed world-wide – list... although I admit the list is a subjective one. Against stiff competition from the Pompidou Centre in Paris and the Guggenhiem Museum in Bilbao, Draycott has what is beyond doubt The World's Ugliest Building. Surprisingly, I've seen many people drive past it, cycle past it and walk their dogs past it without a second glance. Perhaps it's so ugly that the photons carrying its image occasionally just shrivel up and die before reaching the human retina. I am of course referring to the thing on the left of Wilne Road just past the boathouses. I think it's called The Thing.

The Thing is owned by Severn Trent Water and is a river intake pumping station. How can I describe it? As far as its relationship to its environment is concerned, imagine the addition to the scene in Constable's *Flatford Mill* of a Japanese supertanker, and you're in the right ball park. What we had here, before its arrival, were a series of meadows gently rolling down to the River Derwent, where a winding country lane passed a short row of charming cottages before briefly nuzzling alongside the meandering stream. What Severn Trent did was to cover the meadow nearest the river with an enormous and featureless grey breeze-block and surround it with an enormous and featureless grey fence, such as may be designed to keep psychopathic murderers inside. Or outside, I suppose. What the architect might have been thinking when he or she 'designed' it, and what the the council official might have been thinking when he or she passed the planning proposal, is anyone's guess. My guess is that they were both thinking: "I'm getting tired of posing as a human... I think it's time I contacted the mother ship to take me home to the planet Blob."

Seriously, I've no doubt that this installation is doing something useful... though perhaps not quite as vital as the the job of the embankment across the road. This forms part of the flood prevention measures taken after the December 1965 inundation which falls into the category of a 'once-in-80-years' event. At the flood's height, vast tracts of the lower Derwent valley were under water, including the lowest parts of Draycott, all of Church Wilne up to the slight rise in the ground just below the entrance to the bridleway to Breaston (the Coffin Walk) and of course all the meadows between Church Wilne and Ambaston, as well as a great many to the east. The water level nearest Draycott reached 34.82 metres above sea level, the 35-metre contour crossing Wilne Road near its junction with Derwent Street.

The resultant protection measures were planned in 1967 and implemented by the end of the decade. Their most evident feature around here is the flood bank which starts in the back gardens of the houses on the west side of Wilne Road, beyond Derwent Street, continues to form the raised river bank beyond the boathouses and then stretches eastwards almost to Sawley Road. Lest you may think that the flood water has only to 'sneak around the edges', rest assured that each end of the embankment coincides with a natural rise in the ground! In fact, parts of the embankment were raised in 1978. The embankment did its job in Autumn 2000, when the river burst its bank to flood Church Wilne yet again, but at its height was still a few precious feet below the top of the bank near the boathouses.

Other measures taken by the authorities (first Severn Trent, then the National Rivers Agency and nowadays the Environment Agency) have included the installation of flow-monitoring stations, for example the small station just upstream from the weir at Wilne Mills, from which vital data can nowadys be accessed instantly from remote computers. A similar station used to be in operation on the Draycott bank close to the site of the chain ferry and, although this is no longer used, the cable slung over the stream here is a reminder of the flow-monitoring devices that were at one time slung below it into the river. (This is a miniature version of the structure still in use, for example, on the Trent just downstream from the City Ground.) The Environment Agency certainly takes seriously the flood threat in this section of the Derwent Valley and its Land Rovers can frequently be seen on visits to Draycott and Church Wilne. It's interesting that the Agency's early-warning system includes flood warnings to Armiston Cottages, the only remaining habitations in Church Wilne outside the firework factory.

On the map again

On a more positive note, in the late 1990s the old Derby Canal route has re-emerged as one of a number of developments that are finally putting Draycott on the map. While a canal restoration project has for some time been toiling to rebuild and re-open the Derby Canal itself, it has been overtaken by Sustrans, who, with the help of various local authorities and the support of government grants, are putting the finishing touches to a vast new national cycle network, stretching from Penzance and Dover to Inverness and Skye. And Draycott sits bang in the middle of it! The cycle track running parallel to the old Derby Canal forms part of National Route 6, one of the 'Millennium Routes', this particular stretch running from Derby to Nottingham and thence northwards to Yorkshire.

1997 saw the launch of 'The Draycott Village Trail' by Groundwork Erewash Valley, celebrated by a walk around the trail led by Councillor Derek Orchard and available to all as a free pamphlet from Groundwork Erewash Valley.

In August 1999 Draycott's first-ever permanent art gallery opened in the old 17th-century barn on South Street as The Beetroot Tree Gallery. Embroiderer and artist Alysn Midgelow-Marsden and her husband Brian had bought the barn, and the remains of the stable block behind, in 1997, starting refurbishment of the main building the following year. Together with colleague Pat Hazzledine, they run art and craft classes and mount short-term exhibitions on specific themes, displaying works from all over the country but focusing on local talent.

With these initiatives, the success of St Chad's Water (see below) and the popularity of water-skiing and jet-skiing at the nearby Church Wilne Reservoir site (from 1996), could Draycott's future be as the centre of a new leisure zone?

St Chad's Water

By the 1980s, Hoveringham Gravel (later Tarmac Roadstone) had extracted gravel from a series of pits across the floodplain between Sawley and Draycott, an operation whose road vehicle support caused considerable disturbance to local residents. Partly in compensation for this nuisance, Tarmac Roadstone (Eastern) Ltd agreed to sell to Draycott Parish Council in 1984, for the nominal fee of £1, the flooded, used-out pit that now forms St Chad's Water, this to become an amenity for the local community.

In fact, many local groups and individuals – not least the council members and officials themselves – set to with a will to deliver the excellent resource enjoyed today by humans and birds alike. Flowers were planted, trails developed, seats and information boards provided and disputes resolved. Initially wind-surfing had been permitted, but this activity was stopped and angling strictly controlled. At one time, an artificial island was created in the middle of the lake, but vandals destroyed it. Litter-louts are still a menace and volunteers still keep the effects of their thoughtlessness at bay. One of the initial jobs was the naming of the lake and this task was handed over to local school pupils, whose suggestions – apart from the successful and quite appropriate one – included one in honour of the nearby firework factory: Guy Fawkes' Pond.

St Chad's Water is the largest, but not the only lake in Church Wilne, for another legacy of the gravel workings is the partially hidden lake that now extends in an arc beyond the southern and eastern edges of the churchyard.

A turn-of-the-millennium snapshot

And so we come up to date, with the turn of the millennium (which many celebrated a year early on 1st January 2000!). Below is a list of the businesses active in Draycott and Church Wilne on 17th March 2000.

\multicolumn{3}{c}{Businesses in Draycott and Church Wilne, 17-Mar-2000}		
Category	Business	Name	Location
Industry	Textiles	Aburnet	Walter St
		Classic Lace Knitting Ltd	Draycott Mills*
	Textiles??	Official League Merchandise Ltd	Walter St
	Explosives	Haley and Weller	Wilne Mills
	Electrical goods	Venture Lighting Europe Ltd	Victoria Mills
	Other manu-facturing	Paul Fabrications	Town End Rd
		BMR Presswork Ltd	Draycott Mills*
	Engineering	Astec Ltd	Victoria Rd
		Power Press	Draycott Mills*
		Latham Service Engineers	Draycott Mills*
	Catering and distribution	W J Parry and Co.	Town End Rd
Shops	Grocer	Bhalla Foodstore	Station St
		Jacques	Station St
		Barney's	Market St
	Grocer and newsagent	Draycott News	Victoria Rd
	Butcher	G W Dundas	Victoria Rd
	Postal services and stationer	Post Office	Victoria Rd

* Shortly after this survey, a sign was erected officially announcing the site as 'Draycott Mills Industrial Estate'.

77

	Chemist	A Wilson	Station St
	Gifts and promotions	Fiddle Sticks	Station St
		Boston	Station St
	Clothes and bric-a-brac	Treetops Hospice Shop	Victoria Rd
	Furniture	Dovetails	Victoria Rd
Catering	Pub	Traveller's Rest	Derby Rd
		Victoria Inn	Victoria Rd
		Coach and Horses	Victoria Rd
		Olympic	Station Rd
		Rose & Crown	Market St
	Cafe	Webster's	Victoria Rd
	Takeaway	The Famous Chef	Derby Rd
		Good Luck	Victoria Rd
Other services	Business and financial services	Harrison and Co.	Station Rd
		Halifax Agency	Victoria Rd
		Derwent Financial Services	Lodge St
		Michael Aspinall Associates	Victoria Rd
		R F Acton and Co.	Victoria Rd
	Leisure services	Associated Brewery Leisure Services Ltd	Victoria Rd
		New World Leisure International Ltd	Victoria Rd
	Property services	Hickory Gate Properties Ltd	Victoria Rd
	Financial services	G W Baxendale-Baines	Victoria Rd
	Video services	Video Systems (UK) Ltd	Market St
	Motor services	Draycott Garage	Victoria Rd
		Villa Street Motors	Villa St
		Preferred Driving Services	Market St
		D & S Motorcare	Draycott Mills*

		Cee Bee Garage	Draycott Mills*
	Upholsterer	Banks	Sawley Rd
	Art services	Beetroot Tree Gallery	South St
		Studio Ten	Market St
	Pet services	M A Aldridge (Vet)	Derby Rd
		Sally Anne Canine Grooming	Station St
	Hairdresser	Cactus Cutz	Station St
		Unnamed!	Station St
		The Hair Studio	Victoria Rd

The most startling change is the sharp reduction in the number of shops: from 36 in 1953 to just 11 in 2000. In fact, a few months after the above survey, two more had closed (Fiddlesticks and Dovetails) while no more had opened, taking the total down to 9 shops for about 2,800 inhabitants, compared with 36 for 2,227 fifty years earlier. One of the reasons for this – nearby superstores catering to the car-owning shopper – has been outlined above and Draycott's dwindling shop-count is one of the most oft-quoted concerns of local residents. To this has been added a recent question mark over the survival of many local post offices around the country with the possible withdrawal of their service in paying out Social Security benefits.

As far as businesses in general are concerned, Draycott and Church Wilne now have 51 for 2,782 inhabitants (the latest census figure), a 19% reduction for a 30% population increase since 1953. As you'll see from the above list, many of the current local businesses do not serve the village, but rather find Draycott as a convenient (or perhaps cheap?) location for a business that could in fact be located elsewhere. The only 'boom industry' seems to be catering, with most of the five pubs (the same five as in 1953) now offering food of some kind, and the takeaway trade increasing. In fact a planning application has recently been turned down for yet another takeaway in the village.

And what of Church Wilne? Well, it's still there... but only just! The church is still active of course and Haley & Weller are still manufacturing 'pyrotechnics' at Wilne Mills. But the hamlet's housing stock is down to two – four former semis converted into two detached houses, on the corner of the bridleway to Breaston. The latest buildings to be demolished were the farm and cottages on the north side of the churchyard (see photo). As Roy Christian has pointed out, on misty mornings the lane through Church Wilne nowadays has a distinctly mysterious air, not dissimilar to the remote reaches of the Essex marshes.

Alive and well and living in Draycott

Draycott, however, is a socially thriving community. A 2000 roll call of the village's social groups would have included political clubs, slimming clubs, the Women's Institute, pub quiz teams, church groups, senior citizens' groups, the Church Wilne Jetski Club and many more.

Managing many of the local changes is **Draycott Parish Council**, since 1973 forming part of Erewash District rather than Shardlow Rural District. The Parish Council celebrated its centenary in 1995, when a popular exhibition in St Mary's church hall recorded some of the highlights of those hundred years.

Some brief examples of the council's activities in the last quarter of the 20th century show the diversity of its work and the challenges it faces:

- It distributed free beef from the (then) EEC's beef mountain.
- It arbitrated in a dispute over the over-close proximity of certain graves in the cemetery.
- It dealt with applications for a ground survey in the Sawley Road vicinity in search of oil (no significant finds being made).
- It resolved controversies associated with the creation of a conservation area in the centre of the old village. (See map below.)
- It sought the views of villagers on the proposal to build a community centre on the 'leisure area' off Derby Road. (Unresolved at the time of writing.)

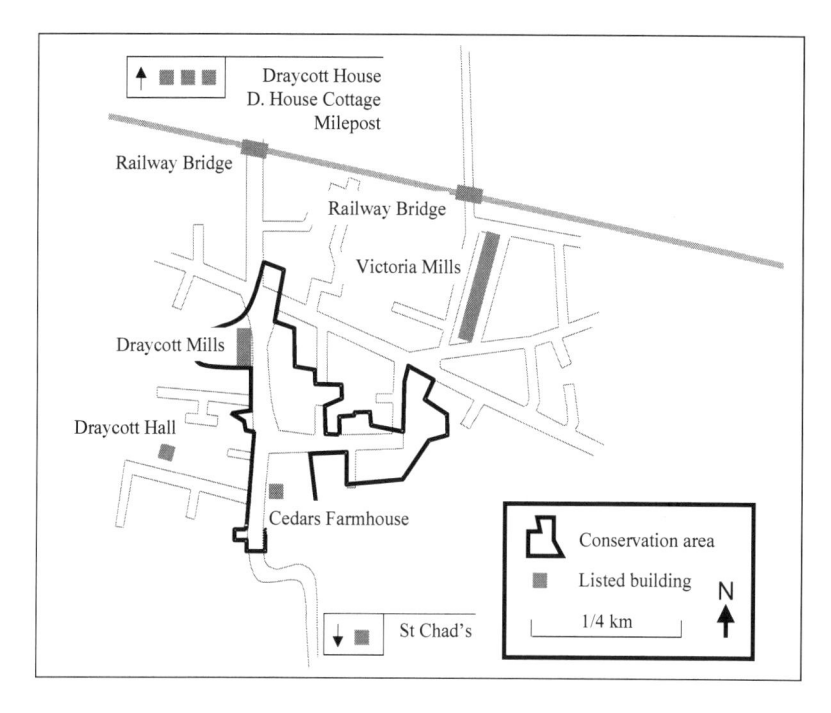

Draycott conservation area (1994) and listed buildings (2000)

Ghost town in cyberspace

All this activity certainly proves that Draycott is alive and well as a community at the turn of the millennium. However, it would seem that in one respect at least it is still half a yard behind the rest of the Western world. At the time of writing, an Internet search on 'Draycott' or 'Church Wilne' will take you to only one website for a local organisation. That's not to say that Draycott's industries don't have their own websites (for example, www.venturelighting.com), just that only one organisation has linked itself to the village name. Do you want to take a guess which one it is? (History Mystery 10: answer towards the end of the book). In fact, as for all towns and villages in the UK, the community structure is ready and waiting on the Internet, with categories such as 'business' and 'recreation' already set up, but – in cyberspace at least – Draycott appears as yet to be a virtual ghost town.

Floods at Wilne, probably 1930s.
Photo: Long Eaton Library

Captain of Draycott Amateurs FC, Ron Mason, receives the 1957 League Cup (Derby Senior League, Section A) from the League Chairman. Draycott Amateurs' chairman, Herbert Hopkins, looks on.
Photo courtesy R. Mason

7. Answers to the 'History Mysteries'

1. The original reason why Draycott is known as Neddytown is believed to have been its role as a changing point for the coal-cart donkeys from the north, before the Derby Canal took over the trade. Even when the coal arrived by barge, it was horse-drawn carts that brought the coal into the village from the coal wharf on Derby Rd (opposite Wharf Lane, now Nooning Lane). Moreover, it is believed that horses and donkeys were once regularly bought and sold on Market Street. As to the alternative reason for the locals being known as Neddies, I can neither confirm nor deny that people born in Draycott tend have peculiarly big ears!
2. The Midland Counties Railway, and later the Midland Railway, already had a station at Beeston and it was thought that the name Breaston in a station name would cause confusion. However, Draycott station did become Draycott & Breaston in 1939.
3. It took 19 years to build Victoria Mills because a large part of it burned down part way through the construction.
4. The Cleaver's Inn was part of the house that stands on the north side of South Street at right-angles to the road, forcing the pedestrian into the street. In fact, in the early 19th century there was yet another inn on South Street, possibly named The Red Lion and situated somewhere opposite the current Manor House, although exactly which building is not certain.
5. Draycott's listed buildings include its two railway bridges (1839, Grade II) and the bobbin-type milepost up on the north side of Nottingham Road, outside 'The Cottage' and marking Derby as being 6 miles distant and Nottingham 10 miles (early 19th century, Grade II).
6. In the plans for the Victoria Mills development, Villa Street was originally named Derwent Street.
7. There was a market on Market Street at least in the late 19th and early 20th centuries, but it was probably more a wakes than a market.
8. The original parish church is St Chad's in Church Wilne.
9. As explained earlier, many people left Church Wilne in this century because of its lack of services.

10. The only (and presumably first) organisation in Draycott or Church Wilne with a webpage accessible via a search on 'Draycott' or 'Church Wilne' is the Church Wilne Jetski Club (established in 1996), at www.kortawse.demon.co.uk/wilne/, where it is advertised as being "in a rural location in the Midlands".

8. Bibliography

Adam, D. (1998), *On Eagles' Wings – The Life and Spirit of St. Chad*, London, Triangle.

Astle, M. J. (date unknown), *Wilne Church*, unpublished.

Astle, M. J. (1925), *The Re-Building of Wilne Mills*. See Burrows, M. E. (1974a).

Barton, J. (date unknown), *Memories of Draycott Over 55 Years Ago*, unpublished.

Barton, J. (1999), *Village Memories*, Derby Evening Telegraph, 5th October 1999, pp 22-23.

Bunting, R. (1993), *Anglo-Saxon and Viking Derbyshire*, Derby, J. H. Hall.

Burrows, M. E. (1974a), *The Re-Building of Wilne Mills*, unpublished. This document is a re-production of a booklet written by M. J. Astle in 1925.

Burrows, M. E. (1974b), *Draycott and Wilne in 1842*, unpublished.

Burrows, M. E. (1983), *Draycott 1761-1861*, unpublished.

Childs, J., (1985), *Tudor Derbyshire*, Derby, J. H. Hall.

Childs, J., (1986), *Stuart Derbyshire*, Derby, J. H. Hall.

Christian, R. (1984), *The Villages of Draycott and Church Wilne*, Derbyshire Life and Countryside, Vol 49, June 1984, pp 24-26.

Christian, R. (1987), *Notable Derbyshire Families*, Derby, J H Hall.

Clay, F. M. (1993), Church Wilne, unpublished.

Cox, J. (1999), *Draycott Station 1852 – 1966*, unpublished.

Davies, A., Davies, J. and Hutton, B. (1999), *Derbyshire 242: Draycott Lodge*, Derby Buildings Record, unpublished.

Derbyshire County Planning Department (various dates), *Listed Building Record Cards*, Matlock, Derbyshire County Council.

Derbyshire Planning and Highways Department (date unknown), *Elvaston Castle Country Park*, Matlock, Derbyshire County Council.

Derbyshire Record Society (1979), *The Nottingham and Derby Railway Companion* (originally published 1839), Chesterfield, Derbyshire Record Society.

Draycott Parish Council, *Minute Books 1895 – 1998.*

Erewash Borough Council (1994), *Erewash Borough Local Plan*, Long Eaton, Erewash Borough Council.

Friends of St Chad's (1996), *Church History of the Parish Church of St Chad, Wilne, and St Mary, Draycott*, unpublished.

Groundwork Erewash Valley (1997), *Village Trails in Erewash: No. 9 Draycott and Wilne*, Sandiacre, Groundwork Erewash Valley.

Jeayes, Derbyshire Charters.

Lichfield Cathedral Visitors' Study Centre (date unknown), *Get to Know St Chad & Pilgrimage Through Lichfield Cathedral*, unpublished.

Page, W., The Victoria History of the County of Derby, Vol I.

Reedman, K. (1979), *The Book of Long Eaton*, Buckingham, Barracuda Books.

Roffe, D. (1986), *The Derbyshire Domesday*, Matlock, Derbyshire Museum Service.

Rowley, T. (1997), *Norman England*, London, B. T. Batsford.

Senior Scholars of Draycott Council School (1953*), A Local Survey of Draycott and Church Wilne*, unpublished.

Slater, I. (1862), *Slater's Royal National Commercial Directory*, London, Isaac Slater.

Smith, S., *A Local Miscellany*, unpublished.

Stafford, P. (1985), *The East Midlands in the Early Middle Ages*, Leicester, Leicester University Press.

Sumpter, D. and Heath, J. (1972), "Victoria Mills – Draycott", in *Derbyshire Miscellany*, Vol 6, 1971-73, pp. 68-72.

Notes

[1] Christian (1984), p. 24.

[2] According to The Derbyshire Record Society (1979), p. 33.

[3] As described in Bunting (1993), pp. 13-14.

[4] Adam (1998), p. 77.

[5] Quoted in Lichfield Cathedral Visitors' Study Centre (date unknown).

[6] From an episcopal manor survey quoted by Reedman (1979), p. 27.

[7] Quoted in Burrows (1983).

[8] Quoted in Smith (date unknown).

[9] Davies (1999).

[10] Quoted in Burrows (1983).

[11] Derbyshire County Planning Department, Listed Building Record Card 8/4433135/013, p. 2.

[12] Quoted by Sumpter and Heath (1972), p. 70.

[13] Burrows (1974b).

[14] Hazel Smith, in Senior Scholars (1953).

[15] Ernest Rice, in Senior Scholars (1953).

[16] Even though the parish is 'Draycott and Church Wilne', the Parish Council's minutes refer to themselves as simply Draycott Parish Council, and so I have used the same terminology in this book.

[17] Draycott Parish Council minutes, 10th August 1896.

[18] Draycott Parish Council minutes, 30th April 1897.

[19] See under Burrows in the bibliography.

[20] Special thanks are due to Joyce Barton, Florence Clay and Derek Orchard for help in compiling this section.

[21] Myra Wilmot, in Senior Scholars (1953).

[22] Clay (1993).

[23] Barry Clifford, Senior Scholars (1953). In fact the school pupils were soon to benefit from that playing field themselves since it had become their own football pitch by 1962, when the present author played an away game there in the Long Eaton junior schools league.

Index

air raids..59
Angles..14
Anglicans..44
Anglo-Saxons..14
Antliff, Dr Samuel..44
Armiston Cottages..73, 75
art gallery..75
Arthur Street..54
Astle, Marcus...34, 47, 53, 59
Astrand Mills...60
Attewell House..59
Axe & Cleaver...9
Beetroot Tree Gallery...7, 29, 75
Bishop of Chester..19, 22
Bishop of Coventry..23
Bishop of Derby..44
Bishop of Lichfield..19, 24
Board School...45, 47
Bonfire Night..56
Booth, Roger...24
boxing..70
bridges..11, 40, 84
Bryan, Joseph and Arthur..35
Bullock, William Ewart..46
canals...28
carnival..56
cars...67
Cedars Farmhouse..30
cemetery..48
Chad..16
Chapel House..6, 30
Chapel, Primitive..44
Chapel, Wesleyan..6, 30, 43
Christian, Roy...9
Christianity..15
church...9, 15, 22, 26, 43
Church Wilne..57
Church Wilne Jetski Club...85
Church Wilne Reservoir...14, 76
Church Wilne, name...20
City, The..48
Civil War...26
Clay Street...34

Cleaver's Inn	7, 84
Cleveland Avenue	48, 54
Co-op	63
Coach & Horses	6
coal	84
Coffin Walk	31
commuting	67
conservation area	80
Conservative Club	35
Cooper, Henry	35
cotton	25, 34
Coulson's Yard	34, 72
Coxon's Yard	34
cricket	69
cycle track	75
Danelaw	18
Derby	18
Derby Canal	28, 73, 75
Derby Road	13, 48, 54
Derwent Street	7, 72, 84
Derwent, River	10, 74
Domesday Book	18
Draicot, Doctor	26
Draycott Amateurs FC	68
Draycott Boxing Club	70
Draycott Council School	8, 45
Draycott Council School, survey	60
Draycott Cricket Club	69
Draycott Gas Company	46, 54
Draycott Hall	30, 72
Draycott Hotel	6
Draycott House	30, 59
Draycott Lace Mill	34
Draycott Lodge	6, 30
Draycott Mills	8, 34, 54, 59, 63
Draycott Motor Company	46
Draycott Parish Council	47, 80
Draycott Primary School	8
Draycott Rovers	69
Draycott Swifts	69
Draycott Village Trail	75
Draycott, name	11, 20
Dungeon Hole	10
Edmundson, Geoffrey	24
electricity	55, 64
Elm Lodge	14

Elvaston Street	35
enclosure	27
fairs	55
ferries	11
Ferristone House	44
Ferry House	12
ferry, chain	12, 57
fire brigade	53
fire, St Chad's	52
fire, Victoria Mills	36
fire, Wilne Mills	53
firework factory	11
flood bank	74
flood prevention	74
floods	55, 74
football	68
fords	11
Fowler Street	46
Fritchley, Mr	8
Garfield Avenue	48, 54
gas	54, 64
Gell, Sir John	26
George III	26
Gertrude Road	54
ghost	32
gibbet	43
gravel	72, 76
Green, The	8, 48
Haley & Weller	60, 79
Harrington Street	46
Harrington, Earl of	7, 23, 27, 43
Hartley, William	26
Haywood, engineer	53
Hibbles and Mellors' Wakes	56
hockey	69
Holden family	24
Holland's Wakes	56
Holly Close	72
Holly House	72
Hooley, Ernest Terah	35
Hoveringham	72, 76
Humphries, Rev Thomas	31
hunting	57
Isolation Hospital	49
Jardine, Ernest	36
Kennedy, John	70

lace	34, 35, 52
lead	13
Lee, Garnet	70
Leech, Sir Edward	24
lighting, street	64
Lime Grove	48, 54
listed buildings	84
Little Chester	13
Lodge Street	6
lord of the manor	22
Madan, Rev Spencer	24, 35
Manor Farm	29
Manor House	29
market	48, 84
Market Place	48
Market Street	8, 48, 72, 84
McNeil Grove	57, 72
Melbourne Mill	34
Mercia	14
Mercie	15
Methodists	43
Midland Counties Railway	40
mills	11, 19
Milner Avenue	72
Morlestan	19
National School	8, 44
navigation	10
Neddies	5, 84
Neddytown	5, 28, 84
New Delight	72
New Street	34
Nooning Lane	11
Normans	18
Olympic	6
Orchard's electrical shop	55, 63
Parish Council	8
Parish Rooms	47
Parry, W J & Sons	37
pinfold	29
prebend	22
pubs	5
Queen's Court	72
railway station	5, 40, 64, 67, 84
rationing	60
Red Hill	14
Red Lion	84

Revill, Alan	71
ridge and furrow	27
river crossings	11
river terrace	10
Roman roads	13, 14
Rose & Crown	7
Sawley	19, 22
Sawley Mill	20
Sawley Road	13
Saxons	14
school	55
school survey	45
schools	44
Severn Trent Water	73
shops	68, 79
Skerritt's Mill	54
Smith, Fred	71
South Street	7, 72
sports	68
Springthorpe, Terry	71
Square, The	8, 48
St Chad	15
St Chad's	31, 44, 52, 59, 84
St Chad's Water	11, 76
St Mary Avenue	72
St Mary's	9, 43, 44
Stanford, John	41
Stanhope family	23, 26
Station Road	6
Sydney Road	46
Tarmac Roadstone	76
telephone exchange	55
telephones	64
Thing, The	73
Thoresby Crescent	59
tithe barns	24
Towle, John	8, 34
Town End Road	35, 46
Town Street	29
Traveller's Rest	8
Trent Lock	14
Trent, River	14, 17
Unionist Club	48
vicarage	44
Victoria Mills	6, 35, 37, 59, 63, 84
Victoria Road	13, 72

Victoria, The........8
Vikings........17
Villa Street........35, 46, 84
wakes........55
Walk Close........72
Walter Street........54
war, 1914-18........52
war, 1939-45........59
water power........11
websites........81, 85
West Avenue........54
Whalley, Richard and Thomas........23
wharf........28
William the Conqueror........18
Wilne Lane........14
Wilne Mills........24, 34, 53, 60, 79
Wilne Road........10, 14
Wilne Toll Bridge........12
Wilne, name........15, 20
Winfield, A........72
Winfield, John........72
world's ugliest building........73

The Author

Richard Guise was born in Derby in 1951, grew up in Long Eaton and attended Long Eaton Grammar School, before taking degrees in Geography and Economics at the University College of Wales (Aberystwyth), and in Transport Studies at Cranfield Institute of Technology. Having tried a variety of jobs including schoolteacher, economist, van driver and freight forwarder, he finally took up a career writing technical material for the computer industry in the 1980s. This led to three-year spells in both France and Spain, plus a short stint in California, before he returned to Long Eaton in 1996, subsequently living on McNeil Grove in Draycott for a short spell. History is just a hobby.

Other Books by Richard Guise:

Lead Us Not Into Trent Station (2003, 2014)
Limerick Gazetteer of Europe (2004)
From the Mull to the Cape (2008)
Over the Hill and Round the Bend (2009)
Two Wheels Over Catalonia (2011)
A Wiggly Way Through England (2013)

Those in stock are available through bookshops, via amazon.co.uk or from the author at richard_guise@yahoo.com.

For up-to-date news on Richard Guise's travel writing, go to www.facebook.com/richard.guise.7 or look up his author page on amazon.co.uk.